LOW DOWN ON THE SLOPES

LOW DOWN ON THE SLOPES

The Essential Ski Holiday Guide

Patrick Thorne

WILLOW BOOKS
Collins
8, Grafton Street, London
1985

To Scamp and Cath, two small hairy people I love very much!

Willow Books
William Collins & Sons Ltd
London · Glasgow · Sydney
Auckland · Toronto · Johannesburg
First published in 1985

Cartoons by Ian Dicks

Thorne, Patrick
Low down on the Slopes: The Essential Ski Holiday Guide
1. Skis and skiing – Europe – Handbooks, manuals, etc.
I. Title
796.93′094 GV854.8.E9
ISBN 0 00 218173 8

Filmset in Apollo by
Ace Filmsetting Ltd, Frome, Somerset
Printed and bound in Great Britain by
William Collins Sons & Co Ltd, Glasgow

CONTENTS

ACKNOWLEDGEMENTS

I would like to thank my parents for starting my skiing career and supporting me in my writing career, and just about everything else. I am indebted to my editor, Louise Haines, for her patient work on my messy manuscript, for her help and advice, and for the tuna pizza. Thanks are also due to my literary agent, Carolyn Whitaker, for her continuing endeavours towards my wealth and fame; and to Alan Smith at Collins Willow for originally realizing just what a smart idea this book is!

Thanks for the inspiration and the fun are due to: Cathy 'Pontoon' Pinder (*Après Ski* Specialist); John Whiting; Penny Robinson; All the Swedes and their moose; The Humphs; The Dellys; Ethel Brooke; One Dick in a Million; Jo Gibby; Ruhi Smith (Spiritual Guidance); and last and least, Ratface. Also all other members of the 007 Mentalski Club and remembering those in the Bilborough Ski Party (La Polsa, Italy, 1981).

I am additionally grateful to the following for supplying information and advice: Ivan Kemp (CDP Services); Sarah Ball (Woodcock Travel); Kevin Warne (Blue Sky Holidays); Anita Wilson (Enterprise Winter-sports); Amanda Dundas (Bladon Lines Travel Ltd); J. Hutchinson (Thomson Holidays); J. La Measurier (Global Travel); Andrew Selby, David Moore and Jeff Garner (Neilson Holidays); Lisa Salonen (Lillywhites); Dinah Holland (Intasun Skiscene); whoever it was that corrected Thomas Cook Travel's entry in the chart showing the services offered by the holiday companies; Sally Spence (Snowtime); Mitch Terleckyj and Andrew Daniels (Alpine Sports); Bernard Gilhooly (Correctamess Inc); and most of all to my bottom for supporting me so often while skiing.

Introduction

As more and more people go skiing you'll find an increasing number of books about skiing on the shelves – so how can I justify writing another? The fact is that all the other books are practically useless to the skier. For instance, there are the 'Learn to Ski' type books (which this is not), there are the ski resort guides (which this one isn't in any detail), and there are the books telling the tales of great skiing heroes (which this one doesn't). This book, however, is a guide to ski holidays. Covering more of your trip than just the brief moments you'll be spending whizzing down the mountainside – this book tells you how to get back up as well! You can also learn about the other types of skiers you'll run into (probably literally) on the slopes, or pistes as you'll soon be calling them.

In other words this book doesn't make the assumption that you've magically appeared on some mountainside, free from all other people and at peace to learn the perfect technique from your English-speaking tutor. It just doesn't happen that way and a book that tells you it does and what you're going to learn is, in my opinion, pointless. It's rather like trying to teach someone to play football without their ever having seen a football or a pitch, let alone run a few feet.

The resort guides are all very well if you're going to spend your time hopping from one to another but otherwise there isn't much use for them. As far as books on ski heroes are concerned you should find the information within these pages far more useful than a list of the top Bulgarian ladies' ski teams of 1926.

This book is not for the armchair enthusiast but for those asking themselves the question: 'to ski or not to ski?' and indeed for those already firmly committed but who want to know more. It gives you the whole ski holiday story from picking up the brochures to picking up your snapshots when you get back.

How it all began

'That's enough for today, let's all go to the restaurant' – these were the words of John Lennon back in 1964 after his first ten minutes of skiing at St Moritz. John was an extremely good beginner and, according to his instructor, possessed natural style; but his comments sum up well the light-hearted approach most people take when new to the sport. Falling over is a large part of the fun in the first few days; you're doing something wrong if you don't come a cropper, and that's as good an excuse as one of John's: 'I only did it to please the photographers'.

When Lennon was skiing two decades ago, skiing was still a luxury sport indulged in by only the wealthy. Since then its expansion has been incredible with all the major tour operators fiercely competing for your custom and plenty of smaller companies besides dealing exclusively in the ski holiday market. That isn't to say that skiing is a low cost sport, it is certainly expensive, especially if you become addicted and buy your own equipment (though this will save you money in the long term). But skiing is becoming cheaper every year, or comparatively so anyway, with the tour operators all trying to establish a good share of the growing market and offering all sorts of discounts and schemes in an attempt to get you to book with them.

Every year there are more innovations which improve the standard of skiing equipment and the new skiwear designs lead sports fashions all over the world. If you walk through a town today, you will see more people than ever before wearing ski jackets (though most leave their goggles and ski boots at home when they are just out for an afternoon's shopping). Every year more ski shops and more ski slopes open, including the dry ski slopes in Britain. Everything that has happened in the ski world recently is very good news for the consumer (unless of course you're rich enough to have been skiing for the past 30 years and snobby enough not to enjoy the invasion of the commoners). The only problem is that the more opportunities and deals there are on offer means more to choose from, more special offers and a lot more to get confused about – and that's one of the reasons why you need this book.

Now, as this is the tale of the typical ski holiday and what you should expect from it, I should really start at the beginning and that's a lot further back than you may imagine. The commercial boom in skiing has happened only over the last decade, though it had been gaining momentum since the Second World War, and skiing as a recreational sport has been around for the last 80-odd years only. It was in 1898 that Henry Lunn took the first winter sports package tour to Chamonix in France calling it the 'Public Schools Alpine Sports Club' and limiting members to those from public schools. In those days it was considered not the done thing for the upper classes to travel abroad in groups, carry guidebooks and cameras or to have luggage

labels on their bags as this made them look like tourists! So, forming a private club solved the difficulty.

Without doubt it was Lunn's ingenuity in beginning these early alpine trips, when so little was known about skiing, which started off the holiday package and indeed helped the sport of skiing develop in the way it has. It was Henry's son, Arnold Lunn, who was responsible for creating the first downhill race in 1923 at the British Championships in Wengen, Switzerland which was a good ten years before the 'rest of the world' began theirs (a good thing to point out when told that continental skiers are so much better than the British).

However, skiing started a long time before the first crazy Brits started pushing themselves down mountainsides with two blocks of wood strapped to their feet. It started 4000 years ago, in Stone Age times, though it is doubtful if they were having downhill races then. Like all of the oldest sports, skiing was born out of necessity, being a means of travelling across land which was covered in snow for a large part of the year – the new fangled wheel was of no use in that sort of terrain. Evidence of early skis has been discovered mostly in Scandinavia, the oldest being found in 1921. Known as the 'Hoting Ski', after the area in which it was discovered, it has been largely saved from atmospheric damage by having spent its time in a bog (minus skier) and has been dated at 2500 BC. Over in Norway at the same time someone (with very good eyesight) was carving pictures of skiers on cave walls. The ski in the bog was found nearly 200 miles away from the rock carving, so unless one early caveman had drawn his self portrait, skied 200 miles, become bored with the sport and chucked his ski into a bog, it is pretty certain that skiing was quite widespread 4500 years ago.

Fifteen centuries later it was still going on when 24 pictures were carved onto the rocks around the White Sea area of Northern Russia. The figures depicted were naked and with the temperatures at minus 40°C, it's safe to assume that unless those early skiers were very thick-skinned as well as kinky, skiing around the White Sea didn't last long. (In his book *The Moon's a Balloon*, ski lover David Niven described the effect skiing in a pair of rather thin trousers had on some more personal parts of his anatomy, which then had to suffer the indignity of being stuffed into a cup of coffee to revive them from frostbite!)

Skiing didn't end with the frozen nudists, however, and indeed they may have been the pioneers of skiing for fun and pleasure instead of out of necessity. For the rest of skiing's history, that's 3000 years, there are many stories of great deeds involving skis such as those of Scandinavian kings being carried to safety on skis where enemies could not follow on foot. And in the nineteenth century a man known as 'Snow Shoe Thompson' was the first to carry mail on skis across the Sierra Nevada in the United States. He made it onto a postage stamp!

However, all that is history and today more and more people are finding that skiing is the best sport they have ever attempted. *Low Down on the Slopes* will hopefully explain to you a little of the ski world and a great deal of the ski holiday market that is now a major part of it. It will advise anyone who knows as little about ski clothing as those nudists from the White Sea area on just how to keep warm and it will advise anyone wanting to start a new trans-Sierra Nevada postal service on where they should buy their equipment, what they should buy, and how they can look after it. In fact all you need to know about your ski holiday and the preparation for it is contained within these pages. So please read on.

BOOKING

Where to go

The two major considerations for those searching for their ideal ski holiday must be where and how much – though not necessarily in that order. Although the holiday companies would like you to believe that the answers to such questions can be found simply the truth is that, in practice, finding the perfect holiday is nigh on impossible. The task could be most closely compared to trying to obtain an income tax refund. To get an accurate idea of the holiday best suited to you, you'd really need a computer programmed with all the relevant information from the multitude of tour operators and the likelihood is that your holiday either wouldn't exist or wouldn't be available. But don't be discouraged! You can still rely on that old mental computer to turn up an excellent choice especially with the aid of this marvellous volume. In any case the most important aspects of a successful ski holiday, such as snow, cannot be prebooked – even though some companies will guarantee it.

If you have already decided where you want to go, you can skip onto the next section which details the elements that make up the total price of your holiday; but for those who are dithering about where to go, here is some information for you.

Which Country?

Although much is made of the postcard image of Switzerland and Austria with their picturesque valleys, chalets and mountains magnificent, the villages of Italy and many French resorts can be just as pleasing in their own way. Similarly, though people may tell you that Switzerland and Austria are terribly expensive, half a litre of beer in a French ski station (the French like to call their resorts 'stations') will cost you nearly twice as much as in the former two countries. The price at £2.20 is amazing when twice that quantity in the supermarket costs only 40p! On this meagre evidence then, I will dare to make the claim that there isn't an awful lot of difference between the alpine ski resorts in any of the four major countries. At least 96 per cent of ski holidays sold in the United Kingdom are for: Austria (55 per cent); France (17 per cent); Italy (16 per cent); and Switzerland (8 per cent). Indeed, drawing a line between some of these countries can be difficult with some vast skiing areas stretching across national borders.

Being up in the mountains, ski resorts tend not to possess very much of their country's national 'flavour' or identity. They are basically tourist resorts and as such will contain a variety of bars, nightclubs and gift shops. Resorts are also generally villages or small towns and the communities within them are close knit. Therefore if a beer costs 80p in one bar, you'll find it costs 80p everywhere else too. There is

often more competition between the restaurants, but the sports boutiques generally agree to be expensive together. Another unifying factor of ski resorts all over Europe is that they're full of skiers from all over Europe and the host nation is nearly always in a minority to the rest of the world.

However, there are some differences between the resorts of each country. Although quite a few of the pretty Swiss and Austrian villages have been built specially for the skier, they still have the monopoly on picturesque chalets and you can still find villages with that genuine 'cow smell' coming from the barns and where the inhabitants walk around in traditional dress because it's Sunday and not because the local tourist office has paid them to do so. If you do find such a resort you're lucky, the more expensive ones certainly won't offer you that authenticity. Look for the plastic air purifiers on the sides of the brick cow sheds to see if you've picked the wrong place.

Many people, perhaps rightly, call cow smells and fancy-dressed yokels 'atmosphere' and complain that the French ski stations don't have any because they have been purpose built over the past decade or so and don't possess any locals, let alone cows. Whether this sort of thing is important to you is a matter of personal taste. I manage to have a thoroughly enjoyable time in France and find there is 'plenty going on' of both an organized and disorganized nature. But for those who like to ramble around old churches and snoop through the other remnants of history, it is true that there is little to be found in most French resorts. It all depends on what you call atmosphere. In Italy many of the resorts are old villages to which a large number of new buildings have been added but in keeping with the style of the old ones. In the Eastern European resorts, little attention has been paid to aesthetic considerations and new concrete hotels have been stuck up where required.

Natural mountain scenery cannot fail to be fantastic, but once again the Austrians and the Swiss have captured the market in the most spectacular. The Matterhorn overlooking Zermatt is pretty awe inspiring and Austria's Ziller Valley, taking in several of the country's main resorts, is equally impressive. Virtually every ski resort you find in the brochures will claim to have breathtaking and beautiful scenery and indeed it's difficult for them not to have it. Not only do the mountains look wonderful from across the valley but the buildings covered in snow with six-foot icicles hanging off them are rather lovely too and this is especially so when you come from a country that manages half an inch of snow a year which has melted by mid-morning. If you ever studied geography or geology at school you will now be able to see real examples of the topics you yawned through on a Friday afternoon – cirques, glaciers and of course those beloved mis-spelt knapps!

As I've said, prices are high in France, Switzerland, and Austria. Italy is markedly cheaper, except for the mountain restaurants which are expensive everywhere, and so is Spain. The cheapest of all is Andorra but the Eastern European countries also offer excellent value. The Bulgarian tourist board was recently offering people an '80 per cent currency bonus' to ski there. This meant that any British tourist who went there was given 80 per cent more Bulgarian currency for their sterling. You will also find that denim jeans can be sold for vast amounts on the black market; but trying these deals is not advisable unless you want to spend your holiday in jail.

Après ski doesn't differ much across the Alps either. In Italy you can get a pizza evening and in Austria a Tyrolean evening, but otherwise you'll find a sledge night, bowling night, fondue party, disco night and torchlit descents pretty widespread. (See pages 96 to 100 for further discussion of *après ski*.) Perhaps the only really discernable differences between resorts are those of their size and their trendiness. For a fuller guide to the resorts, look at some of the specialist resort guides.

Skiing

It is on the slopes themselves that the resorts vary the least. Snow and mountains are very similar wherever you go and so the only real difference is between the steepness of the runs and the size of the skiing area. For example, some resorts may have only 10 kilometres of prepared piste with just one difficult run while the biggest resorts are often interlinked to give hundreds of miles of piste with a large selection of run types, as well as having 'off-piste' skiing available. The more experienced skiers will probably need the choice and size of the larger resorts but beginners will be perfectly happy with and not so overawed by a small resort. Another important consideration is that lift passes, ski hire and tuition are likely to cost much less in a small resort than in a big one. For instance, you may pay £90 for a week's pass and equipment in a large French resort but perhaps only £35 for equally good equipment and unlimited use of the lifts in a smaller resort, you'll just be using the same lift more often.

Teaching Techniques

There are a few catches, however, to this 'stay small and save money' policy for beginners which mainly concern teaching techniques. The traditional way of learning to ski as taught at most ski resorts is on relatively long skis. First of all you are taught how to slow yourself down by using the snow plough: pointing the tips of your skis together, pushing the ski heels apart, and tilting the ski's inside edge inwards. Having mastered that, you are then taught parallel skiing which is the 'proper' way of skiing and which relies on leaning the body, transferring your weight and keeping your skis together, you therefore have to unlearn snow plough!

In certain French resorts, however, *ski evolutif* has been introduced whereby complete beginners are put on skis only 1 metre long (the normal minimum length for adults is about 1.6 metres). They are taught parallel skiing techniques from the very start as the short skis are so easy to control. The *evolutif* lessons last all week and depending on your progress, classes will be moved onto 1.3 metre and 1.6 metre skis during the week. This method is undoubtedly a far faster way of learning than the traditional method and it is available at some of the larger French ski stations such as Les Arcs. Look at your brochures for details of others.

However, Les Arcs is a good example of a gigantic resort with expensive lift passes and six days' *ski evolutif*, including tuition, lift pass and ski hire, will cost about £100. Having said that, when I took some complete beginners with me to that resort, they were skiing some of the steepest slopes with complete competence after a week's *ski evolutif* training. The only problem being that with such short, soft skis they fell over on the flat!

Accommodation

When choosing your holiday destination you will also have to decide on what sort of accommodation you want to stay in. You will find some differences here between countries. Italy will offer you mainly hotels and a few apartments. Austria and Switzerland will give you a choice of hotels, chalets and pensions. The last-named are sometimes called 'snow hauses' or 'snow houses' in brochures and provide bed and breakfast. Accommodation in France mainly comprises large apartment blocks with the odd, and normally expensive, hotel and some chalet holidays.

Some of the least expensive accommodation is found in the Swiss and Austrian guest houses which offer you a 'comfortable', though some would say slightly spartan, room with private facilities available at slight extra charge. The buildings themselves, though large chalet types, can accommodate up to ten or fifteen guests only so if you want a swinging 'group' atmosphere these are rarely the accommodation for you unless by some miracle you all get on. Rooms are usually twin-bedded. The beds often seem to be two singles that have been nailed together to form a double with a ridge down the middle to prevent any naughtiness happening with any comfort. The beds also tend to be short, as do the quilts that cover them, so remember to take some bedsocks if you're tall, unless you sleep in a foetal position. If there is a group of more than two of you travelling together, the French apartments begin to become more economic. These will take up to six people but there are a few smaller ones and they offer extremely high-standard accommodation in most cases with fully-equipped kitchen facilities, including even a dish washer, separate bath and shower and lavatory. The six-sleeper will have bunks and convertible sofa beds in the main living area and then a separate bedroom containing the remaining two beds. There's also plenty of space and far more freedom than in any other type of accommodation. The apartments do, however, have the same problem as most other skiing accommodation – little or no provision for drying wet skiwear and it becomes more noticeable when six or more of you all pile gloves, socks, salopettes, hats, jackets, jumpers, shirts, scarves, and other items onto a three-foot wide wall heater. There is usually a clothes horse too.

Although there is obviously a great price range between those already mentioned, the next up in cost is probably the hotel holidays in Italy or Eastern Europe. These will offer you half-board in basic hotel accommodation. Hotels have their own bars and sometimes their own discotheques which will save you a lot of money if you like them, as discotheques in the resorts are notoriously expensive. It really depends on whether or not you want a prepared evening meal or whether you like being more flexible. In a hotel you can relax after a hard day's skiing before going down to dinner, whereas in an apartment you can walk in and start cooking whatever you fancy or just collapse in the shower assuming that no one has got there before you.

Chalet holidays are the traditional skier's accommodation – a sort of giant apartment with waitress service by the celebrated chalet girls. So chalets are a sort of cross between the freedom and group atmosphere of the apartment and the service of the hotel. They are also more costly.

Top of the range are the first-class hotels which are found everywhere but are concentrated in Austria, Switzerland and France. Although these appear the most expensive, you will normally pay a reasonable price for what you get in return. Hotels will offer you half-board as full-board is of little use if you're on the slopes all day and if you can afford to stay at one of these hotels you will be able to afford the mountain restaurant prices.

A general thing to look out for with all accommodation is any reference in the brochures to just how far it is from the bottom of the slopes and the lifts. It's no joke having to carry heavy ski gear across town, especially when you're wearing ski boots, so beware of: 'just ten minutes' walk from the lifts' as that could mean a mile uphill and you'll be exhausted before you even start skiing.

The Weather

The right weather is of course essential to a good skiing holiday but really there's not very much you can do about it, especially when you're booking half a year in advance. Many of the resorts in the brochures are chosen for their good weather conditions. In skiing terms this means a lot of snow falling at the start of the season, the sun shining every day until May, except of course in the middle of the night when more powder falls. But the temperature should never drop to below freezing point so the snow doesn't become too hard. Well, that's the theory!

Another interesting theory was put forward by a ski guide for a major company whom I talked to during one of the big ski shows in London. He maintained that the snow was coming later each year and by the end of the decade ski holidays would run from January to May instead of from December to April – which would certainly be a shame for those of us who like to go away for Christmas and the New Year to avoid all the horror of those events at home. Indeed it wouldn't do anyone in the ski business much good as that's the time when prices are bumped up most to enable vast profits. However, the ski guide changed his prophecy when I pointed out that I was going to his resort, with his company, from 14 December for a fortnight.

Seriously though, it is very difficult to predict weather conditions. The general rule is that most snow falls at the start of the season, literally changing resorts from dry to 'three feet under' in a matter of hours. If you go early in the season you are gambling on whether there will be snow but assuming you have a snow guarantee, there's little to worry about because you get to ski the new snow first, the crowds are fewer so you can ski more freely and in greater space and sometimes the hire equipment is new. I have also skied in mid-April when small amounts of snow were still falling but on the whole the thaw was well under way with the streams in the villages at bursting point and the villages themselves completely free of snow. It's a rather interesting experience to travel up in a lift from a lovely village to a snow-topped mountain in ten minutes. So the start and end of seasons can be just as enjoyable as all the weeks in between.

Finally, always remember to accept bribery. Not only holiday companies but travel agents are at each other's throats in a desperate bid to get you to book through them. At the most it costs nothing to use a travel agent so you'd be pretty foolish not to, especially in the complex ski market and with the price of using a phone these days . . . no, I haven't been bribed by ABTA. But more than that there's offers of free insurance, free shopping vouchers plus a multitude of other gimmicks available to the ski holidaymaker who shops around.

The cost

Skiing is expensive, there's no argument on that point, but it is also great value according to those that indulge and who will willingly sacrifice the conventional summer holiday for the winter fun. One week hurtling through fog and snow showers certainly beats lying on a boring sandy beach for three, your nose will turn red either way so you may as well enjoy yourself in the process.

So, what are the real costs? Well, you'll know that in all holiday brochures the 'basic holiday price' quoted in a dates and accommodation cross-reference block at the bottom of the page does not give you the full price – as airport fees, insurance and so on are still to be added as well as the dreaded surcharges. Ski brochures are just the same but far, far worse and the real cost of the holiday is often nearly double the basic price. So you must be careful to include everything. As well as the basic cost of your holiday there are many optional extras which you can take up, such as snow guarantees by which the operator undertakes to take you to a different resort or give you a refund up to a certain amount if there is not enough snow for you to ski on at any time of your holiday in the resort you're staying in.

The following will give you an idea of what to look out for when you wade through the brochures in search of the ideal holiday.

Thc Basic Price

Obviously this will depend on what type of accommodation you choose, where you go and when. Many companies offer self-catering apartments (usually in France) or 'snow houses' which are guest houses giving bed and breakfast only (usually in Austria or Switzerland). You will need to allow extra money for the unprovided meals with these though it usually works out cheaper than going to one of the generally expensive hotels. See page 18 for more details of the different types of accommodation available.

The high season for skiing varies to some extent from resort to resort but it usually includes Christmas and New Year and then prices soar again during February, March and April. Generally, the cheapest time to go is during the week or so before Christmas and the week or two after New Year. You are perhaps gambling slightly on the presence or quantity of snow if you go on the earlier dates but prices are a good deal cheaper and the slopes a lot less crowded (giving you more space to ski in and less time to spend queuing for the lift). So these are worth aiming for if you have a limited budget.

Transport

Most basic holiday prices include air travel but it is often worth considering coach travel which can save you a good deal of money and will often take little longer than flying with not so much messing about or so many delays. The price of coach travel may be given in a separate fare table or you may just have to deduct £30 or £40 from the price by air shown in the normal table. Particularly luxurious coaches are operated by Neilson (Snowcoach), Global (Skiliner) and Enterprise Holidays.

Some companies will not offer very good coach services – you can get a good idea of the standard of the coach from the brochure photographs and the facilities listed alongside. Just see which company can boast the most. Another advantage of coach travel is that it may pass nearer your home so you won't have to spend so much time getting to and from the coach station as you do to the airport. Coach tolls are usually lower than airport taxes too. See pages 32 to 36 for a fuller discussion of different types of travel including going by car.

Flight or Coach Supplements

Normally detailed in the small print beneath the basic price block. Additional charges for those of us unfortunate enough to live north of London and thus having to travel further. They should be included on your invoice and are payable in advance.

Airport Taxes or Coach Tolls

The authorities grasping their little bit of your money.

Lift Pass

The first of those unique ski extras, which is essential to enable you to get back up those mountains that you've just whizzed down. One of the obstacles to improving your skiing ability is that you have to spend more and more time on the various lifts – though at least you're getting more value for money. A rotten trick adopted by some brochures is that in holidays where you have to pay for the lift pass in the resort they give you the price in foreign currency. First-time skiers may not, therefore, fully realize the costs involved which are frequently as much as £50 for six days. In any case beginners should look around for the 'inclusive' packages which offer tuition, equipment hire and lift pass all in one; as the companies and resorts scramble to catch the increasing numbers of new skiers there are still bargains of this type to be found.

Equipment Hire

The hire, rather than the purchase, of skis, boots and poles is sensible on your first two or three trips. Once you have become a regular skier, investment in your own equipment will work out cheaper in the long term. Borrowing from a friend is also a possibility but ski equipment is very individual in that it should, in length and type, match not only the height and weight of the skier but also the ability and the style of skiing preferred. There is really no such thing as a multi-purpose ski and slalom skis are very different from racing skis as are the boots. Hire equipment is suited as much as possible to the conditions, your physique and to standard – the hire also usually adds between £20 and £40 a week to your expenses.

Again, watch out for prices quoted in foreign currency. Although the companies give these foreign prices in order that, or so they claim, the prices are not affected by currency fluctuations after the brochures have been printed, I think it would be a lot better if they converted the prices to sterling and then stated the date of the conversion and rate of exchange. This way the prices could be checked back if need be, rather than your having to make constant conversions to compare total holiday costs. I cannot stress enough that a basic holiday price of, for example, £150 combined with a £50 lift pass and £30 ski hire (total £230) can prove more expensive than a basic holiday price of £180 with a £30 lift pass and £15 ski hire (total £225) and such price differences for ski equipment and passes are not uncommon from resort to resort and especially between countries. The best company

I have found for not giving prices in foreign currency is Thomson and you can often book lift pass, ski school and ski hire in advance with them (only boots need to be paid for in the resort and are quoted in foreign currency).

Ski Tuition

Vital for beginners and, in those early weeks, also useful for intermediate to advanced skiers who can stand having their style verbally ripped apart in front of them by a professional to stop them developing bad habits and to prevent them becoming cocky. Such abuse costs money, however, but once more you are talking of between £20 and £40 a week. So you will be lucky to get skis, lift pass and tuition for under £70 a week and in France the costs were around £100 a week in the 1984–85 season.

Insurance

Let's face it, there's no such thing as a decent insurance company. There is not an insurance company that exists where the small print isn't the standard text, the text is incomprehensible, and even when it is comprehensible it's totally ambiguous. Most travel companies have arranged deals with leading insurance companies which they recommend you to take up. The details should be studied as carefully as possible and will generally read something like:

'Blah, blah, blah, £750,000, blah,blah, blah. All medical expenses covered, blah, blah, blah, blah, blah, blah . . .' until you've forgotten what it is you're reading. Then in small print: 'except all accidents occurring while on ski lifts, racing or doing anything other than skiing downhill at less than 1 mph with full and complete protection and without malice aforethought as is, has been and ever shall be, till death do us part, blah, blah, blah etc.'

Insurance does have to be taken up in some form or another of course; you are more likely to be injured while skiing than when you are lying in the middle of the beach and for that reason the costs are slightly higher. Look carefully at exactly how much cover your policy gives you and try to ensure that it is as comprehensive as possible. Some people with a little extra money to spend, invest in two policies to lessen the chances of being ripped off should the circumstances arise.

However, most insurance policies are pretty similar, both in price and cover, and the one recommended by your tour operator should be sufficient. Companies will usually either recommend a particular policy and insist that you pay for it or, occasionally, include insurance in the price. If you are travelling without a tour company, it's always best to get comprehensive cover from a well-known company and your travel agent should be able to advise you on the technicalities. Prices in the 1984–85 season were around £10 for a week and £17 for two. For some reason policies will normally provide cover for nine or seventeen days which isn't the length of the average holiday! Special insurance policies offering exceptional cover are available at an extra cost and you should ask your travel agent if interested.

On top of insurance, you would be wise to get form E111 if you are going skiing in France or Italy. This form is available free, usually over the counter, from your local DHSS office. It entitles you to the maximum discount or to free medical treatment in most EEC countries and some other countries. The medical treatment you will get is detailed in form SA36 which you'll get with E111. You should apply between one and six months before departure, if possible.

Group Discounts

It's often more fun to ski in a group and, if you can get a large enough group together, most companies will give you a discount when you all book together. The discount comes in the form of a free place if you can manage to get ten or twelve people to travel together. If you can muster more forces, the free places will be more though these usually depend on departure dates. In the high season, for example, you may get half a free place for a group of ten only whereas if you travel mid-January you may get one free place for the same number.

The free place will apply to the basic price of the holiday only but this will still mean at least 5 per cent off the total cost of each person's holiday or at least £10 off which can mean an extra five bottles of wine each on the last night!

Children's Discounts

Most companies will allow children under the age of two (or 'infants') to travel free on their parent's lap. Otherwise discounts for children are many and varied depending on the time in the season, the type of accommodation and availability – the earlier you book the better. Children must normally be under twelve to qualify.

You should also look out for the companies which offer children special facilities in the resort; being dumped in a ski school full of foreign terrors with no one else who can speak English (including the teachers) isn't most under-twelves' idea of heaven. Some companies operate their own children's ski school or kindergarten for the very young which are totally British-run and full of British kids (what could be more delightful!).

When companies do offer limited free places for children, remember it is almost invariably the basic price that is free and all the extras such as insurance, lift pass, and ski hire have to be paid for though these should also be at discount prices.

Surcharges

The hated holiday term which means that they bump an extra 10 per cent onto your final invoice. Thankfully these dirty deeds are becoming less frequent so look out for 'No Surcharge Guaranteed' on the front of brochures.

Transport Costs to and from Local Airport/Coach Station

Whether you travel by aeroplane or coach, you may well find yourself quite a distance from the departure point, so look out for companies which offer optional free or discount return travel from your home to the airport or coach station. For instance, Global offers discount rail travel to London (and free to those living in the home counties). Without such discounts, the additional costs can be at least another £10 return per person. It all adds up.

Snow Guarantees

What every skier dreads is arriving at the resort, having spent a substantial sum of money in getting there, only to find nice grassy hillsides and a distinct lack of the cold white stuff. Snow guarantees are therefore extremely useful because first the company undertakes to take you to the nearest resort which has skiable snow or, failing that, it gives you a refund for each day without snow – at some cost to the company. The amount of the refund varies (for example, Thomson pay £15 a day, Neilson £20 a day) but the most important factor is the guarantee whenever possible to take you to the nearest snow because no refund could make up for no skiing on that long-awaited holiday.

Learner's Guarantee

Most ski companies offer discounted 'learn to ski' weeks for first-timers which give you a chance to find out what skiing is all about. These are certainly well worth taking up if you haven't skied before because not only will the resort have been chosen for its suitability to the first-timer but also the holiday company will be going out of its way to be nice to you and secure your future business. On top of that there will also be a lot of others of your own standard falling over with you when you may otherwise get left out while the rest of the ski world whizzes past you.

Few companies, however, are brave enough to put their money where their mouths are and guarantee your enjoyment. Neilson will offer a £50 refund in certain resorts to those who find they don't like skiing after two or three days. In the promotional blurb about the offer in the brochure they cautiously state: 'We're glad to say that not many people took us up on our offer last year.' Of course £50 back doesn't make up for the overall financial loss and your own disappointment at finding out that you are one of the minority that doesn't enjoy skiing – but it's a damned sight better than nothing.

Early Booking – and Payment – Discount

Some companies, such as Inghams, offer 5 per cent discounts if you book and pay for your holiday by mid-August before you go away. Although this looks like a bonus for those who have the money in the bank ready to pay, the 5 per cent is severely worn away in the lost interest on the money you've handed over so early. If you were travelling in December you may lose only two months' interest as most of the other operators would want the balance paid by mid-October but if you are travelling later in the season the saving becomes minimal. So once again, better than nothing but not a lot!

Package Deals

Not too many of these about nowadays but you may still be able to find a company which offers a discount if you are flexible about departure dates, hotel, resort or even country. Certainly worth considering if you are very flexible but you could miss out on many of the other discounts (such as those given for children) mentioned earlier and so these losses should be weighed against the package deal savings.

Seasonal Specials

With Christmas lying midweek for the next couple of years, these bargains are hard to find but some companies do offer special seasonal trips which can be a few days longer for little extra cost. The companies involved will try and pretend that this is because their only goal is to give you maximum enjoyment but it is because most holidays have weekend starts and with Christmas or Boxing Day falling on a Friday or Saturday, the transport services will be closed down. So they have either to take you early or late or you won't get out there. Even if the transport services were still operating, no one wants to travel on Christmas Day (unless the price is right!).

Filling the Apartment

In France, the apartment price per person will vary depending on how many people you can cram into it. If you can get six in a six-sleeper chalet then you will pay the minimum price for the time of season you go. Otherwise, if you have four in a six-sleeper chalet for example, you will have to pay around a £30 supplement per person per week. Of course you are able to breathe for that extra cost. In other types of accommodation, you may find extras such as single rooms and private facilities available for a small supplement as with normal hotel booking.

Beginners' Ski Packs

These include such things as *ski evolutif* (gradual ski length increase) which is available in some resorts and through some companies and is what the French consider to be the best way to learn to ski. *Ski evolutif*, and other beginners' ski packs, can offer substantial discounts on the standard prices for a combination of equipment hire, lift pass (not always necessary in the first few days) and tuition (very important initially).

Going it Alone

Although the previous sections are to a large extent general to all ski holidays, they are based mainly on the complete ski holiday package offered by the major tour operators. It is, of course, possible not to travel with a tour operator but to go it completely alone, making your own accommodation arrangements and getting there under your own steam. Most national tourist offices will advise you on accommodation (see page 115 for addresses). Otherwise many companies offer air, train or coach travel to various resorts, leaving you to make your own accommodation plans. Many also offer standard discount for those who wish to drive to their resort but who want to book their accommodation through the company. A few companies, such as Horizon, offer an almost complete individual service where they will attempt to book you into any hotel you fancy so long as it is advertised in their brochure.

I have been skiing completely under my own steam, having bought a discount rail ticket to Switzerland, stayed at a youth hostel and hired my own equipment. However, that was in mid-July for the summer skiing and I merely stopped off *en route* to somewhere else. From a cost point of view I would always choose the complete cover of the ski holiday package during the winter but in the summer I think I'll go on my own again. It all depends on your preferences and your purse. However, you should always try to get as much information on prices and places as possible from the tourist offices before you go.

The Final Decision

No one can pretend that there isn't much to think about in that little lot though certain travel companies may try! Whatever you do, don't be put off by the variety and number of things you need to consider. Quite simply, the more elements the ski package holiday has to it, the more holes there are with pots of gold, or money-saving offers at least, awaiting you at the bottom.

Unless you have a lot of time to spare you would do best to pick up three or four brochures which you think are most likely to contain the holidays you want, then have a nice leisurely read through, making a note of those that interest you. When you have decided on your top five or so, work out the advantages and disadvantages of each, then put it to a vote (assuming you're not travelling alone). Go down to the travel agent armed with the brochure containing the most free offers but keep a second, third or fourth choice in reserve just in case some rotter has already booked it. In other words don't spend weeks comparing prices and trying to find the holiday that offers everything I've mentioned. There is so much to choose from that you're bound to end up with a good holiday.

The brochures mainly come out in June or July and you should try to book early, that is, by September, especially if you're going during the high season such as over Christmas. I'm not saying this to endear myself to the holiday companies that would love you to book early, but because I know that there is nothing more annoying than getting a list of five holidays sorted out and finding them all booked. Your travel agent is unlikely to be able to suggest alternative ones – he'll want you to quote him a holiday rather than asking him to do it for you – and he won't know all that you require. As with all holidays, you can make late bookings and ask your travel agent what's available but, unlike summer holidays, there are rarely any savings to be made and the lack of choice may mean that you end up with something totally unsuitable.

In the long run, though, you can't lose. The only thing you can do wrong is not to book at all. And if you put off skiing for another year you'll live to regret it. 'To ski or not to ski?', that is the question. You've got to do it sooner or later so you'd best start now.

How to go

Undoubtedly the most popular method of travel is still by air, followed not too closely by the increasingly popular coach trip. Some companies also make provision for those wishing to drive to their resorts, and of course you may also choose to take the train. Each type of travel has its own advantages and disadvantages but I've mainly listed those of flying and going by coach as that is the choice given in the majority of brochures. A few companies, however, do allow you to make your own travel arrangements, while booking your accommodation for you, and so some information is included for prospective motorists.

Air travel is undoubtedly the fastest means of getting from A to B, but there are certain problems attached to it. Flight times, for example, may be at such an early hour, or returning so late, that it becomes necessary to book into a hotel before or after your holiday (assuming that you live some way from your departure airport). Then again, travelling in the winter months increases the chance of delays or diversions because of poor weather conditions. Aeroplanes don't like snow, unlike most of us. Other time eaters include the safety margin that you need to leave to ensure you reach the departure lounge by the time specified and also the 'transfer time' from your destination airport to your resort. In other words the 90-minute flight will probably be less than a fifth of your total journey time when travelling by 'air'.

However, that's not so long as the coach which usually takes about 24 hours allowing for breaks and ferry crossings. Many people have bad impressions or awful memories of long distance coach travel, but this image is being gradually improved with the introduction, over the past few years, of genuine 'luxury' coaches. These buses have wonderful suspension systems which make the journey very smooth. They also contain videos, fridges, hot drinks machines, toilets, reclining seats, good heating and air conditioning. Other than that it is up to the travel company itself as to the service it provides on the journey. Some manage to pick totally unsuitable videos to show and are completely disorganized when it comes to seating arrangements. Others manage to create a no-smoking area and offer blankets for the overnight stretch of the journey though the particularly comfort conscious may like to take a small cushion of their own.

Having experienced the best and worst of both coach and air travel, I can say only that my worst ever experience was by air when I flew with a large group of friends to a small Italian resort. On the trip out we had to leave home at 4 a.m. meaning that we lost that night's sleep anyway. We then had to spend hours waiting for the plane which was delayed, only for it to be subsequently diverted 400 miles south from our destination airport. The next night was spent waiting for the transfer bus to arrive from our original airport destination followed by the drive north in terrible conditions sitting three to a seat on the decrepit Italian bus. So the entire trip took nearly 30 hours, we lost a day's skiing and were totally exhausted for the rest of the holiday.

However, I have had bad coach journeys too. The real advantage of the coach is its comparative cheapness and the fact that most companies place no restrictions on luggage weight. So if you're going to be self catering you can cart out a few cardboard boxes of food to sustain you while on holiday. If food stocks and economy are not so important to you, you probably won't consider the coach for very long unless, of course, you happen to get air sick.

You won't find any brochures offering train travel as part of their package except for the discount schemes on the cost of your journey from your home to the airport and the odd special national railways brochure. It is possible to travel by train if you wish. Several of the national tourist offices listed at the back of this book are agents for their national railway systems and will be able to offer you full advice on train times, ticket prices and so on, to any destination you care to mention. Obviously it's often a problem carrying your skis around and you may be charged a supplement so you should inquire about this when you write to the tourist board; some travel agents may allow you to go by train while arranging your accommodation for you in advance but there isn't a great deal of advantage in travelling by train unless you're going to a resort not covered in the brochures.

Taking your own car offers the independent skier tremendous flexibility, and a number of the large companies capitalize on this desire. Blue Sky and Thomson will arrange accommodation in the

resort of your choice, while you make your own plans for getting there. Inghams will book your ferry tickets for you but Global go the furthest offering ferry tickets and AA 5 Star Service Insurance which covers all aspects of international travel insurance, though you will need personal insurance too.

Although you will save a good deal in air fare, petrol is expensive these days so the more people you can fit into the car, the better. Of course the real value of travelling on your own is that you can stop for a few days at other resorts or towns on the way down, or travel to nearby resorts to test the skiing in other areas once you have arrived at your own resort.

There are several important practical points to remember when driving to mountainous areas including:

- Drive on the right!
- Always take snow chains; these can be hired from motoring organisations such as the AA, ordered through garages or car accessory shops, or bought in garages abroad
- If you're taking your own skis, you will need a roof rack. To comply with international law, your bindings should be covered and the tips of the skis should be at the back and facing downwards
- Make sure you've got a strong solution of anti-freeze in your car before you go
- Make sure you have full international car insurance such as Europ Assistance (Green Card)

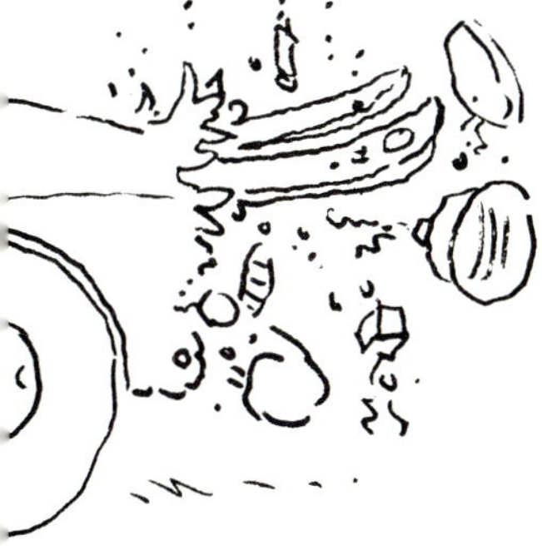

■ To be legal in Europe you need to take: an advance warning triangle; first-aid kit; fire extinguisher; beam deflectors for headlamps; a spare tyre; GB sticker; and in Italy a left-hand wing mirror. You must also have spare bulbs for your lights in France which is advisable anyway, spare spark plugs, contact breakers, a fan belt and coil. Also, don't forget a small shovel, windscreen scraper, a torch and a windscreen protector for when leaving your car outside at night in below freezing conditions

■ When leaving your car outside it is advisable to lift the windscreen rubbers away from the windscreen and, if you are parked on flat ground, to leave the car in gear with the handbrake off as this is liable to freeze

■ Take any other documentation you can think of: the handbook; your driving licence; car registration documents; MOT certificate if applicable and so on

Now, you're all ready to go!

BEFORE YOU GO

What to take

What you need to take:

- Waterproof top, preferably with a high neck
- Waterproof trousers or ski pants
- Two pairs of thick woolly socks (to alternate)
- Ski goggles (and ski sun glasses if you wish)
- Two warm sweaters, preferably with a high neck (to alternate)
- Thin polo neck sweater, thermally insulated useful
- High altitude facial protection cream
- High altitude lip protection stick
- Woolly hat (and head band if you wish)
- A scarf will usually come in handy
- Ski gloves or mittens (waterproofed)
- You will probably need a passport-sized photograph for your lift pass

If you are staying at an hotel over Christmas or Easter it is advisable for men to take a shirt and tie and for women to take a dress or skirt as special meals may be laid on where more formal dress is preferred. And coach travellers who take their own cushion for extra comfort *en route* can become the envy of all others; though most companies provide blankets and the coaches have reclining seats, cushions are the missing luxury.

These then, are the essentials. I cannot stress enough that it is a complete waste of money to spend a lot on purchasing these items if it is your first trip. A ski holiday is expensive enough without spending another £100 or so on clothing or a fancy ski suit when an old anorak and cagoule trousers will normally be quite satisfactory. On top of the waste of money, you'll look extremely silly walking around in the posiest clothing on the slope when you are unable even to stand up on a pair of skis. The best idea is to borrow if possible and perhaps buy the essentials such as goggles, gloves and sun creams which are reasonably priced anyway.

It goes without saying that you would be very unwise to buy skis and boots before your first trip. It is not only a terrific risk buying

equipment for a sport you're not certain that you're going to like but, more importantly, you won't know what sort of skis you will want. A good salesman in a ski shop will be able to discuss the pros and cons of a range of ten skis for a good two hours because there is no such thing as an 'all-purpose ski'. Before you go, you won't know which one you want (even if the salesman knows which one he wants to sell you).

In addition to the above list you may find it useful to take some *après ski* boots which are usually the large 'moon boots' or the ones that look like (and probably are) sawn-off mammoth's feet – apt for vegetarians. A pair of wellies will do just as well if you're not set on being trendy.

If you do buy ski clothing you will probably find it is cheaper to buy it from the large chain stores rather than from the specialist clothing and equipment stores for skiers. You may, however, find less choice at the former and don't be surprised if everyone else on the slopes is dressed in the same way as you. The best time to buy ski clothes or equipment is undoubtedly at the end of the season and during the close season (April to September) when prices are cut as demand is down and the shops need to sell off old, but good, stock before the new styles come in.

The emphasis generally is on warm and colourful clothing. Until you become the next Franz Klammer the ski atmosphere is very much a fun-packed one so take a lot of holiday clothes, the sort you wouldn't be seen dead in at home! Take as many clothes as you can manage as it's all bound to get soaking wet after the first snowball fight and drying facilities are usually sadly lacking.

Health and fitness

Skiing is an excellent way of improving your general fitness and many people talk of feeling 'bionic' on their return. However, you will get a lot more out of skiing if you are as fit as possible before you go. It is important to start exercising a good few months before you are due to leave and build up gradually because a sudden burst of activity prior to departure will leave you only exhausted when you get on the skis. It can also be worth while asking your doctor's advice on your general level of fitness and just what you should or should not be doing.

Skiing is certainly an extremely physically-demanding sport and the major elements of fitness required are: endurance (muscular and cardiovascular); strength (muscular); flexibility (strong powerful muscles are no good if they don't bend as the skier has to); agility (they need to do it quickly too); and co-ordination (they all need to work together). Not much to ask for really and, oh, remember you'll need

to be able to relax your muscles after testing their other abilities to the full.

General fitness is all-important so recommended exercises which you should take up gradually are: jogging or running; swimming; skipping; cycling (this provides endurance and strength and one of my ski tutors once likened the weight transfer involved in skiing to riding a bike); stretching and relaxing (such as touching your toes and trunk rolls).

Circuit training is also highly recommended and almost universally applicable, regardless of age, sex or level of fitness to a large extent. It is a British invention (fanfares!) and was designed to develop all-round fitness for both professional and amateur athletes in many sports including skiing. First of all you must warm up with loosening-up exercises such as some of those already described and arm swings, small jumps, running on the spot, press-ups, box jumps, (jumping sideways over a box) and so on. These are all elements of circuit training which you will have probably experienced during PE or gym lessons at school. You should make a record of your progress, pushing yourself to, say, one more press-up a day, but not pushing yourself so hard that you feel you are going to kill yourself.

For the masochistic one of the best leg exercises is to lean against a wall as if in sitting position. Then just stay there as long as you can. For extra agony you can always hold your arms out horizontally at the same time.

It is a good idea to look at any book on general fitness or even one of the specialist ski fitness books of which there are several. Better still, join an exercise class whether it is one specially for skiing or just for general fitness – you will find that exercising in a group is a lot easier than exercising alone in the same way that dieting, giving up smoking and so on are, except that with exercising there is nothing wrong with doing a little extra on the side.

At the time of going to press, there is no need for any vaccinations if you are going to one of the major European alpine resorts, but keep away from St Bernards that foam at the mouth – the barrel of rum is just a ploy!

Dry ski slopes

For a full list of dry ski slopes in Britain, please see page 116.

I think it is fair to say that there is a great deal of controversy over the effectiveness of learning to ski or trying to improve your ability on dry ski slopes (see, for example, the review of *How we Learned to Ski* on page 127). There is no doubt that dry slope skiing can be useful experience but I personally think, in many cases, it is vastly overrated. There is also the danger that many new skiers may be disillusioned after trying the highly-recommended dry slope skiing when the only similarity between skiing on an artificial slope and skiing on snow is the movements.

Before I went skiing for the first time I took six 'one hour per week' lessons at my local dry slope and I certainly enjoyed it particularly as I was with a group of silly schoolfriends! But when we did finally get out to the Italian Alps the difference was amazing as our skis were longer, we were moving faster, turning was much less of an effort and the snow was far less painful to fall on. I won't say that our dry slope tuition put us at a disadvantage to those who hadn't tried it but we did have to spend a few days adjusting to the different conditions. And we certainly didn't find ourselves with a huge advantage over those putting on skis for the first time.

I didn't venture near a dry ski slope for the next five years, not because I had anything against them, or underrated their value, but because I didn't live very near one and wasn't keen enough to make the effort. When I next spent half an hour on a dry slope as part of a promotional evening for a holiday company, I didn't enjoy it one bit! I was out to impress my friends who were, theoretically, supposed to be less advanced on snow than me. So much for my ego! I was the first one down the 20-metre slope and was the first to fall over much to the amusement of my friends. They were in the beginners' class on the other side of the slope and were spending their first five minutes on skis compared to my five years' experience.

The instructor told me that I had to greatly exaggerate my movements as the artificial surface was much slower than snow. My second descent was slower and more controlled, so slow and controlled in fact that I kept stopping because I was unable to turn out of my turns. I reverted to snow plough and spent the rest of the evening trying to relive my days of learning to ski on a dry slope five years earlier.

However, this is just my opinion and being honest I have to say that I don't find dry slope skiing very enjoyable. I don't feel that I can really improve my technique on it and I don't experience any of the exhilaration of snow skiing. Many people would disagree with me and a lot of serious skiers in Britain spend much of the closed season practising on dry ski slopes. The movements are certainly the same as in snow skiing and you are exercising the correct muscles and parts of your anatomy – so it's worth trying dry slope skiing just for that. Besides you may enjoy it. As an incentive to booking your holiday, most tour operators will offer you discounts on dry ski slopes once you've booked with them.

I should also say that the dry slopes I have skied have been under 60 metres long and were made out of the most common type of surface called Dendix. Many artificial slopes are considerably longer with varying gradients and they are made of much more modern materials which, I'm reliably informed, are easier to ski on.

So I certainly recommend that you try dry slope skiing but, if you haven't skied before and find you don't enjoy dry slope skiing, don't be put off the real thing. There is a hell of a difference between falling over on a rough surface one rainy Sunday in Guildford and falling over in the snow on a picturesque mountaintop in Gstaad – you haven't got so far to fall for one thing! There's also no comparison between collapsing in the pub afterwards and looking out over dreary housing estates and collapsing in the mountain restaurant and looking out across the mountains or down to the matchbox-size village in the valley.

Further resort and skiing information

Once you've paid for your holiday, bought or hired all your equipment, spent several months getting superfit and had some practice on the local dry ski slope, you may think that there's not a lot left to do before you catch the aeroplane or bus south for the winter. And you'd be quite right!

However, there is an abundance of information available to the skier before he departs which may be of use to you and could make a great holiday even better. To start off with, there are plenty of books, some of which are described on page 127, which are worth looking at for ski tips or for further information on your resort.

Secondly, you might like to ask your travel company for more facts and figures about your hotel or resort and they are usually able to provide this. You might also ask other companies that use the same resort or hotel for their views on it (though of course you wouldn't say that you had already booked with someone else).

Thirdly, you might try writing to the national tourist office in London of the country you are visiting, requesting resort information. They'll usually send you a nice big map and a detailed street plan. As well as this, the tourist office will normally provide you with lots of other bumph on travel, shop and bank opening hours and so on which you would never have thought of asking for but which can be extremely useful. The Swiss Tourist Board is the best I've come across for providing a mass of information – all completely free of course.

If you're particularly conscientious you may wish to sift through all these hand-outs before you choose your holiday but usually it is the extra statistical information that many of us thrive on, rather than anything that might affect our booking choice.

There are also a number of ski magazines which start coming out in the autumn and continue throughout the season. These include: *Ski International*; *Ski Magazine*; plus Ski Club's *Ski Survey* and *Ski Special*. You can't miss these magazines as they've all got a 'ski' prefix.

You may also wish to join the Ski Club of Great Britain (SCGB), especially if you become a committed skier (for address, see page 114). At the time of going to press, membership was £7 a year which included a subscription to *Ski Survey*, access to the SCGB's London club house as well as the services of resort reps working especially for the SCGB abroad. You should write to them for full details of services and membership application procedure.

Shortly before you go, and all through the ski season, your travel agent should be able to give you snow reports on your resort as these are sent back by most companies each week. These include reports of fresh snowfalls, the depth of snow, snow type and general weather conditions. You will of course be informed of the weather and skiing when you are *en route* to your resort but there's usually not a lot you

can do about it anyway so the point may be lost. Snow reports can also be found in the information sections of most daily newspapers.

Apart from these snow reports the national and local newspapers are tending to devote more and more space to articles on all aspects of skiing. I tend to find that these are often over-generalized resort reports (due to limitations of space) or items on fashions or new equipment. Skiing often makes the news and at the start of the 1984–85 season there was wide media coverage of the lack of snow in the Alps. However, the banner headlines of 'No Snow' were far from true in most resorts but it made good press at the time; disappointing for those about to go away and infuriating for those who had to explain to deaf old grandmothers that in fact there had been snow after all. Though snow was certainly less plentiful than normal, there was plenty to ski on in most resorts. So read between the lines and look out for the articles written by the experts. The *Daily Mail* has regular skiing features throughout the season and the *Sunday Times* seems to be paying more interest than previously – particularly to high fashion on the piste.

The only other things to look out for are the ski shows, your local ski clubs and the ski travel companies' promotional evenings and so on. The most famous exhibition is the *Daily Mail* Ski Show which is held every November for about ten days at Earls Court in London. This show gets bigger each year and it's now been running for more than a decade. During the two months before and after the ski show there are other shows up and down the country which help to whet the appetite. The ski season officially lasts from December to April but is really prolonged throughout the year by the release of the brochures in July, the summer sales of old stock at the stores and then the exhibitions.

So, there you have it, all the extra information there is, I wouldn't advise you to go over the top and get it all, but you will find a lot of it useful and interesting.

How much money to take abroad and how to take it

This is the nasty bit of the holiday – when you've already paid for your holiday but find you still have to pay for your lift pass, ski hire and ski school which can be as much as £100 a person a week. Most companies will let you pay for your lift pass in advance and some will also let you pay for ski hire and ski school though you'll usually find that you have to take out that bit extra for the ski hire. If you are staying in self-catering accommodation in France you will obviously have to take enough to cover your eating expenses, plus £50 deposit between you in case of breakages or missing items in the apartment. On top of that you'll just have to make a guestimate of what you're going to want to spend on food and drink, pressies and postcards.

The most highly-recommended means of taking money abroad is, of course, travellers cheques which you can purchase from banks, some building societies, the post office and large travel agents. You can buy travellers cheques in either sterling or in the currency of the country you are visiting. You may not have to pay any commission when you cash foreign currency cheques but you will lose out if you cash any unused ones when you come back; sterling travellers cheques will cost around 1 per cent to exchange. Travellers cheques are obviously a lot safer than cash and the banks like them because they earn extra commission. Remember to order your travellers cheques about a week to ten days before you go.

For the more flexible traveller, there are two ways of taking money abroad thanks to advances in the world of plastic cards. Firstly, there is the eurocheque card by which you can cash your normal personal cheques abroad at the prevailing exchange rate. The great thing about eurocheque is that it can take three weeks and sometimes even longer for the cheque to be debited to your account. So, if your finances are stretched when you're about to go on holiday (especially over the Christmas period), this is a good way to pay. You need a special eurocheque encashment card and with some banks you also need to buy special eurocheques. The second, even more flexible, friend is the good old credit card and especially Access and Barclaycard which are taken just about everywhere in Europe and that includes most places in the ski resort. You can use them to buy goods abroad and to obtain cash.

If you get really desperate, most tour operators have arrangements which allow their local reps to cash personal cheques with a British chequecard, though this is viewed as something of an emergency measure. Equally drastic is a bank transfer which involves, usually, phoning your home bank and getting them to transfer money to a bank in your resort. This takes time, costs money and you may only be allowed to do so if your account is in the black.

Ski fashions

Given the choice between a ski suit costing £2500 from a top London ski store and a ski suit costing £40 from a department or chain store, which one would you choose? Well I suppose it would depend a lot on whether you'd just won the *Daily Mirror* Bingo wouldn't it? If you do find yourself dithering over prices though, you'd better stay clear of ski fashions because the price range goes on and on into the sky, which certainly isn't the limit.

Actually there isn't too much problem for most of us with an average bank balance, that is, an overdraft. To be fashionable on skis, and in the world of *après ski*, you need to spend hundreds of pounds on kitting yourself out and for the casual skier that's a waste of money. Even though more and more ski fashions are becoming fashionable, making it perfectly acceptable to wear your ski jacket and even your new 'jean like' ski pants off the slopes, the expensive styles are just not worth buying. You can buy a very adequate ski suit for under £50 from one of the major clothing chain stores. If you want something a bit more flash, wait for the summer sales when everything too bright for anyone to buy before Christmas will be down to £60 for quick sale. That's the good thing about fashion, if you follow it you waste a lot of money and look like everyone else but if you stay behind, you save a small fortune and can also claim that you are ahead of it.

There is sometimes some uncertainty as to whether it is better to buy a jacket and salopettes or a ski suit. In terms of price, ski suits will nearly always work out cheaper as these start at about £40 and usually look more stylish than a jacket and salopettes which will cost at least £60 or £70 in total. The ski suit is often warmer as there are less gaps for the cold air to penetrate. Suits are generally slightly less wind resistant if that's important to you! However, the ski suit is generally impractical to wear off the piste in the evenings so you will need to take a warm jacket or coat out with you. Ski suits are also a pain when you go to the lavatory! The other problem with the suit is that when it's very hot you can't just take your jacket off, you will have to strip off from inside to stay cool. But as mountain conditions change very quickly, that's not advisable.

On the piste you will find far more people wearing jackets and salopettes than ski suits and most officials will be wearing the jacket combination. However, on *Ski Sunday* the downhill racers all wear skin-tight suits for extra speed, so the choice is yours.

The research into ski clothing fabrics is becoming increasingly complex. Thankfully manufacturers are paying just as much attention to

the practical aspects of the clothing as to how pretty they look. More advanced insulating materials and laminated fabrics have removed a lot of the bulk from ski clothing while making it warmer still. I think it's something of a shame because people won't look half so cuddly and I don't know if falling over in this thin stuff will be so comfy either. The thinner fabric does, however, allow more freedom of movement and therefore less excuse! The emphasis is on dressing in layers to give an effect not dissimilar to cavity wall insulation or, in other words, lots of thin thermals piled on top of each other rather than one big thick woolly. An example of the thermal material used is Gore-Tex which breathes and is waterproof (but not a duck), while a filament material commonly used is Thinsulate (so named because it's thin and insulatory). The two can be found working together in a wide range of ski clothing within the middle price range, that is, 'realistic' prices which are higher than the economy class but lower than the level at which you start paying for fashion rather than warmth or comfort.

So whatever happened to the good old British black pants, bobble hat and Arran sweater? Well if that's what you've got, they'll suit you down to the ground or down to the bottom of the slope as the case may be. There's no point looking like £2500 if you can't ski like £2500 – you just look like an overdressed idiot. So dress to your standard and no higher, the same goes for the guy who buys super boots and skis before he has learnt to ski – he just looks a complete fool.

One of the best innovations of recent years in the *après ski* market has got to be the moon boot. These hugely practical and very comfortable boots are now on their way out of fashion so now is the time to buy them as they cost less. Like most 'old fashoned' ski wear, the boots are big and soft and are being replaced by more stylized and certainly slimmer boots which you are able to wear back home without feeling stupid. Still, this dilution of ski clothing, and making them multi-purpose, takes away some of the magic for me . . . I mean the fact that you go away and put on big and bright clothes for a week or two before returning to rainy Britain really adds to the holiday atmosphere. I'm just an old sentimentalist at heart.

Headbands are a good idea and though you can pay £40 for one if you want, you can still get a multi-coloured one for under £2 in England. These will protect your ears from sunburn on a hot day, help hold on your sun glasses and yet not let your head overheat as a woolly hat might.

Gloves come very cheap in pvc but make sure you get some thermal inners to go with them. Otherwise a pair of leather gloves for £10 to £18 is a good investment (thermal inners make them even better); after that you are basically paying for style.

Goggles are now completely out of fashion except in snowy weather so don't waste more than a fiver on them. The thing to have is a pair of shatterproof sun glasses which are either held on right round the back of your ears, or have a safety strap to prevent them falling off. You can pay over £100 for a pair of 'I wouldn't know there was anything special about them unless you told me' sun glasses, so pay between a fiver and a tenner. It is quite likely that you will find that the shatterproof theory is wrong or your glasses will be lost or borrowed permanently, so they are definitely not worth investing in to excess.

So the message with ski fashion is that if you want to be noticed, don't follow fashion in a sheep-like way, just be different. The pictures the holiday companies use to brighten their brochures are not so much the rich kids in the smart gear, unless they are extra silly, but more likely someone wearing a parrot on his head or sporting a jacket with 'on the piste again' splattered across it. You can be as rich as you like but you need more than money to buy originality.

Purchasing your own equipment

You will be most impressed to hear that I have risked life, limb and, more importantly, my Barclaycard credit limit to bring you this section. So please make the most of it.

Before we start on a general slog of do's and don'ts, here are a few of the basic rules:

- Never buy equipment for your first trip unless you have money to burn
- Always buy your equipment in Britain
- Always buy your equipment from a specialist ski shop (not just a sports shop unless it is one with specially-trained staff)

■ Try not to exaggerate your skiing standard when explaining to the sales assistant exactly what type of boots and skis you will need; ninety-nine per cent of skiers think they are better than they are (the good sales assistants will allow for this at least). Remember that you will improve faster with skis and boots of an intermediate standard if you are intermediate than you will if you buy advanced standard equipment which you cannot properly control

■ Listen carefully to the advice of the sales assistant. Try to avoid the temptation of buying a ski which is aesthetically pleasing but buy the one he says is best suited to you. (As there is little price difference between the skis in each standard, he cannot sell you the most expensive one for the sake of a better commission)

■ For the best deals you should always buy between April and September, that is, after one season has finished and before the next one begins and the new equipment is brought out

'It is not easy being a ski salesman,' is what they cry in the specialist ski stores and I can well believe it. What can they do when people come into the shop wanting a pair of pink skis to match their new ski suit or a new pair of skis just like the ones their friends had last year. Buying ski equipment is just not as simple as that. The handing-out of skis in the hire shop may seem quite random (and unfortunately sometimes is), but when it comes to purchasing skis and boots from a reputable dealer you are severely restricted by your size, weight, ability and style. You are probably limited to a choice from fewer than five pairs of skis and two pairs of boots in the shop – often less.

The price difference between boots and skis of the same standard will be virtually nil. Prices in equipment, unlike clothing, really differ only according to the skiing standard they are suited for. In other words, equipment for beginners and intermediates may be half the price of that for advanced skiers or experts.

Boots

So out of skis, boots and bindings, you may well wonder which is the most vital piece of equipment. Well it is your boots, then your bindings and finally your skis. I must say I was surprised to learn that when I first started thinking about buying my own equipment. It is obvious, though, when you think about it because all movements begin in your legs, or they should do, and if a boot isn't properly fitted the movement will not be correctly transmitted from the boot to the ski.

On top of that, boots are the place where you will feel any discomfort should they fit badly, so buying the ones which fit you best and keeping to them will help prevent sore feet. Comfort is the chief priority and when you try them on in the shop, remember to wear one pair of thick socks or two pairs of thinner ones; most people take about half a size larger than their normal footwear. Hired boots can not only be uncomfortable but they can also impede your progress. Most skiers and salespeople I talked to said that they bought their boots after their first or second holidays and many left the purchase of skis and bindings for a few years more.

The progression from beginner to advanced in both boots and skis follows a reasonably similar pattern, that is, from soft to hard. When you first begin skiing you will find that the boots and skis you use are soft. Well, though they may seem pretty damned hard, believe it or not, the equipment you are using is soft with easy flex. This means that they are more 'forgiving' and if you make a wrong turn or movement it won't be reflected as much in your skis as it would if your boots and skis were harder. This means that there comes a point when you don't want 'forgiving' boots because you are so in control of your movements that you will need equipment which will respond directly to your moves rather than giving you the chance to correct bad ones. This leads up to expert standard where boots are so rigid and tight fitting that they'll respond to a twitch of your little toe which is what you'll need when you're a few hundredths of a second away from winning the downhill on *Ski Sunday*.

Skis

The rigidity of the boot, however, does not have the same effect on your skiing as a hard ski, in fact almost the opposite. Whereas a rigid boot creates quicker turns, a harder ski will be more difficult to turn than a soft one. This is why when you try on a ski the assistant will often test the 'flex' of the ski by pushing the tip end of the ski down to make it bend. While a beginner's ski will give way reasonably easily, a more advanced ski will not be nearly so easy to bend. The sales assistant will, in any case, be able to bend a ski which seems as hard as iron at least 40 degrees further than you can manage because they know how to do it!

As you become a more advanced skier you'll want harder skis so that you don't curve into any hollows when you're travelling at higher speeds. On the other hand, beginners will want soft skis so that the skis will respond easily to turning without their having to apply more pressure to make a snow plough turn.

After you have decided on the stiffness of the ski, you will need to work out what type you need for the style of skiing you prefer. For example, stability and strength are important for racing skiers while the ability to carve turns well is important for giant slalom skiers or for those who enjoy mogul skiing. Once again this involves the flex of the ski but the length, shape and thickness of the ski also begin to play a part.

There are currently four main types of skis: mid-length, sports length; recreational full length; and competition series. The type best suited to you depends largely on where you fit into the products under all the criteria explained above. The length of your ski will be determined largely by your height and weight but beginners and intermediates will normally start off on mid-length skis which are designed to be about head height in length. Sports and recreational mid-length skis will suit most standards of skier and obviously the longest skis are the competition series models which are designed for advanced or expert skiers. Of course there are exceptions and 'high performance' mid-length skis are said to be capable of keeping even an expert happy.

As for the 'different ski type for different types of skier', it's extremely impractical for most once- or twice-a-year skiers to buy a ski exclusively for racing or just for slalom or moguls. Many skis are therefore suited to most varieties of skiing, or at least if you buy a pair best suited to racing at intermediate standard, they won't break your legs if you try to ski moguls with them even though another pair may have been better for that type of terrain.

Bindings

Talking of breaking legs, it's high time we moved onto bindings. Bindings, often called 'safety bindings' which they only are if they're properly adjusted, are the bit which hold the boot to the ski and vice versa. They are extremely clever devices and will normally cost as much as the boot which usually isn't much less than the skis!

There is a slight paradox in binding manufacture because bindings have to be designed to release the boot from the ski at the first hint of trouble and yet at the same time the skier could be in more trouble if his skis were to come off during a bit of rough skiing than if both boots were nailed to the ski. Bindings are constantly being modified and improved with manufacturers attacking the problem from both ends, developing things like sensory switches which will help to release the boots during rough skiing but won't loosen their tight grip completely until the pressure on them is such that a fall is obviously occurring. Turntables at the heel end of bindings help to alleviate the danger of twisting your leg or ankle, allowing your boot to turn with your ankle or leg.

However good the binding, though, the most important safety factor is its setting. Bindings are set according to the 'din range' which is worked out mainly through a combination of the skier's ability and weight. You should be able to pull your boot out of a binding while your ski is being held to the ground by jerking your knee and lifting your foot upwards. If you apply strong enough pressure it should release the boot. You should also be able to kick, or have kicked, your boot sideways out of a binding. These simple tests ensure that your binding is not too tight to stop it releasing your boot during a crash. At the same time you don't want your binding to be so loose that you can just step out of it nor for it to come off at every turn.

It is therefore very important to have your bindings fitted and adjusted by someone who knows what they're doing, that is, usually by a specialist in the shop or by a qualified ski teacher or similar. You should not alter your bindings unless qualified to do so and you should have them checked regularly. You should also try the simple kick and step-out tests at least once a day while skiing.

Ski Poles and Bags

Besides skis, boots and bindings you're going to need a few other items of equipment. Ski poles or sticks are pretty essential and you'll find a selection of these starting at about £15 a pair, which will be good enough for most skiers. Stronger poles are more expensive. The length of the pole you will need is easy to work out in the shop; let your upper arm hang by your side and hold your forearm out in front of you as if you were holding a tray. This is the correct way to hold a stick and so it is easy to measure the height of ski stick you need after allowing extra for the thickness of your boots and ski.

You will also need bags to carry your skis and boots which are often large enough to take most of your possessions too. The larger ski shops sell their own make of bags which generally cost less than those made by the equipment manufacturers. You may also consider buying a small rucksack or 'bum bag' which fits around your waist like a large purse belt and in which you can carry such on-slope essentials as lip salve, chocolate, catapult for shooting poseurs and so on. Boot bags shouldn't cost more than £10, bum bags not much more than £5 and you should be able to get a good ski bag for £15, sometimes even £10.

Where to buy Equipment

As ski equipment design becomes increasingly complex you will not be surprised to learn that computers are beginning to play a large part in not only the manufacture but also, at the better ski shops, in accurately working out the best ski gear for the customer. At one such shop

I was told that in the near future they expected to be issuing some sort of guarantee to skiers on the safety and suitability of equipment based on computerised records of what the customer told the salesman at the time of purchase, the equipment sold and the settings fixed on bindings and so on. Though such a guarantee is still a little ambitious at present, as well as largely cancelled out by the essential winter sports insurance, there is certainly scope for it in the future if the trend continues towards more and more sophisticated designs.

It is because of the necessity for understanding exactly what you're buying that it is imperative you buy British. That isn't to say that you must buy British skis and boots – you'll be extremely hard-pressed to find any – but you must buy in Britain. Even if you see a really good end-of-the-season bargain in an alpine ski resort, you may discover the day after purchasing it that it is not exactly suited to you; it is at this point that the charming old man who sold you the skis twelve hours earlier will pretend he has never seen you in his life before and refuse to exchange the skis. Of course, there is the chance that after buying your skis in Britain, you cart them out to Italy or somewhere with two weeks' skiing in front of you only to find you don't like those skis either. There's not a lot you can do about it until you get back but at least there is something you can do about it when you get back. There's no communication problem back home and you stand an infinitely greater chance of buying the right pair of skis and boots in any case.

This rule doesn't really apply to clothing purchases, and in Austria you can claim your VAT back if you spend more than £40, so it's worth while looking around the ski stores for bargains. Make sure that you know the going prices at home, though, first because even with no VAT resort prices can be extortionate.

The best time to buy equipment, like clothing, is during the closed season – after the end of one season and before the ski shows open at the beginning of next year's season around September time. The end of season sales usually run into the summer sales shortly before the flood of brochures, new fashions and new equipment hits the market. It's extremely unlikely that the skis, boots, or fashions, will change sufficiently for you to be missing out from one season to another so you're best advised to buy when it's cheap.

Probably the most important criterion for buying skis is to do so at a specialist shop. As the ski industry continues to grow in this country there are a lot more of these shops around and there is usually at least one in every major town and city. At the same time, though, some quite reputable sports shops, and quite a few not so reputable, are adding ski equipment to their product ranges. However, these shops don't always have fully qualified staff who can advise the skier on the equipment best suited to him and if so are to be avoided.

Many people will travel to London to buy their equipment where there are some of the biggest ski stores and the best selection of ski equipment in Britain. The big stores often provide 'ski packages' offering suitably-matched skis with bindings at good reductions, free poles and so on; such deals are worth looking into. The big stores are all represented at the *Daily Mail* Ski Show where they flex their ski market muscles at each other across the hall. You won't find much competition in price there, however, as they all sign an agreement against undercutting.

You can of course buy second hand but it is wise to have prospective purchases checked by someone who knows what they're looking for and there aren't many such people about. This could be why second-hand sales are less common except through reputable dealers who often offer trade-in facilities.

Care of Equipment

Ski equipment is expensive to buy and to make your investment worth while, you must keep it in tip-top condition. The most important thing to do is to wax them regularly. If you want to do it yourself, most ski shops sell a range of waxes together with the spatulas and scrapers to apply them with and these items are relatively inexpensive. You can also buy sprays to protect your bindings and some shops stock plastic film which you can stick over the tops of the skis to protect the paintwork from the inevitable scratches in the lift queue.

Many ski shops will completely 'overhaul' your equipment and this service is fairly reasonably priced. The shops have machinery for smoothing the base of the skis of which the 'crystal glide' stone grinding system is the best available. Most shops, however, have a wet belt system which is almost as good. Like most things to do with skiing, you will probably find the prices for maintenance services are cheaper in the summer. One final thing, store your skis and boots in a cool place during the summer, otherwise the plastic may be affected.

A Final Point

As a final point on the purchasing of gear, there is a tendency among manufacturers to attempt to blind you with science; and reading a number of the brochures you may be left wondering just who has got it right. Here are two typical examples from two different brochures, for two competing types of ski boot which I'll just call 'blue' and 'red'.

> 'The rear entry, three piece shell is closed by two constant leverage buckles which provide an easy and immediate adjustment to fit around the whole foot. But it is when your foot is in the Blue Boot that the technology for the perfect fit takes over. Blue Boots Inc have developed an advanced air system which controls the foot around the forefoot-instep area. A small pump built into the shell inflates a unique bladder system to gently cushion the instep of the foot with an even pressure. Together with an integral release valve, the air system offers an instantly adjustable fit for day long comfort.'

But the opposition feel differently . . .

'A rear entry boot will give you a quick fit that feels OK in the ski shop, but since the closure is in the rear, the boot can't grasp the front part of your foot. Your foot just goes into it, as it would go into a container. The addition of an air bladder helps you hold in the instep, but not the sides of your foot. Pulleys and wires attempt to solve the problem, but they really can't. The best they can provide is an approximate fit. Once you've made the decision to go rear entry that's the price you must pay. Which is why Red Boots Inc don't make a rear entry boot.'

So there you have it. As a mere purchaser you don't know who to believe, you also won't get the chance to test them out unless you're very lucky, though a few holiday companies do offer weeks when you can test out a variety of equipment free.

THE RESORT

Life in the resort

After stepping off the bus on arrival in the resort, you should pause for a moment to sniff the pure mountain air before entering your hotel, snow home or whatever – don't stand near the bus's exhaust or the moment will be ruined! Then you must march into your accommodation with a smile on your face and displaying a friendly manner towards everyone. If the rooms seem smaller than they did in the brochure, or a high-rise block has been built next door to your picturesque chalet since the brochure photo was taken in 1968, don't complain about it. Complaining about things that no one can do anything about will do nothing but get you down, so grin and bear it. Things will usually be all right anyway and you'll get a few nice surprises as well as the odd horror.

Don't bother organizing yourself, by unpacking everything, as soon as you arrive. Instead you should start taking a look around the accommodation or even the town to see what's what or where's where, as well as taking the opportunity to chat to anyone unfortunate enough to be standing alone. (Never stand alone in a ski resort or you will always fall prey to some friendly tourist.) In other words you should break with the routine as much as possible and start having a holiday as soon as you can.

If you're staying in a chalet it's important to get on the right side of the chalet girls. These young girls are often selected from literally thousands of applicants and are chosen for their willingness to work hard for a small weekly pay packet, their good humour, personality and ability to fend off lecherous male skiers (sorry ladies but due to some twist of fate there are no male chalet maids – or very rarely). The chalet girls will know more about the resort than anyone else – or all the interesting stuff anyway. So you may as well pick their brains, over a drink of course, which you'll buy them as the investment of friendship and alcohol will pay dividends at dinnertime, if you're lucky.

You'll also have to spend some time touring the local bars and restaurants to see which one offers you the atmosphere, cuisine and price that you're looking for. It's always fun trying. The biggest price trap in the ski resorts, though, is undoubtedly the discotheques. If the disco is free to get in, check that the tonic water will cost you less than £1 before you buy a round. Otherwise discos usually charge a lot to get in. Hotel discotheques are often the best idea as they usually close at midnight or before and few can survive a long night of drinking and dancing after a day on the slopes and with another day coming up in so many hours.

In the more traditional towns the bars will vary from a few tables in the general store, or combined restaurant bar to something not unlike the British 'Fun Pub'. Prices will also vary accordingly. If you haven't checked already, find out the shop opening hours; these are often from early morning till about midday with a couple of hours for lunch

and then they reopen until about six in the evening. There is often half-day closing and extra holidays at Christmas and other times so self caterers especially should be wary about being left without food. Check the bank times too of course. Another thing worth discovering on your first night is just where the lift stations are and how you get to them. If you have to get the bus, find out where the stop is and the times.

Otherwise make friends with your neighbours and enjoy yourself in whatever way you see fit. Most skiers will judge their resort by the skiing which is quite natural. If the skiing is bad, whether because of the general standard of the slopes or the conditions, the resort's standing will suffer in your opinion. Although you can to some extent work out what a resort is like from the brochure description, look out for key words like 'quiet' and 'peaceful' if you want a bit of life in the evening. But the atmosphere in the resort is of course seasonal. There's something magical about snow, and when the snow melts in the towns below the mountain pistes, some of the atmosphere invariably goes. However, that's at the end of the season when there aren't too many skiers about anyway, clubs are shut altogether and of course all the other winter sports such as sledging, cross-country skiing and curling are over too.

Even if you are disappointed with your resort, you should also always try to make the most of it. You don't really have the excuse of the inaccuracy of the brochure as you should learn to read between the lines. No brochure will actually lie but facts can easily be stretched to make hotels and resorts sound much more inviting than they may be.

Starting to ski

Your very first day on skis and snow will be full of many new sensations and feelings. You'll find out a lot about snow – how hard it is, how cold it is, how wet it is – and related to that how well padded, insulated and waterproofed your ski wear is. There's no getting away from it, you are going to fall over. Everyone comes a cropper and if you don't you're doing something wrong! It's also extremely useful to fall over as much as possible (you can quote me on this to your ski instructor if you want an official excuse), so that you lose your fear of it because you will soon find that, provided your skis are fitted properly, you can do yourself little harm. Some of the positions you find yourself in will also be extremely entertaining. By the end of the day the topic of conversation won't be on who can ski the best but rather who managed the most spectacular or original crash.

You will also probably feel that you're absolutely useless compared with some of those you see whizzing by you from more advanced groups. Well, that's true, but learning to ski well enough to stay up long enough to make some turns and even get down the average slope without falling over, is a matter of days (often hours) rather than weeks. In any case, learning to ski is great fun and I can honestly say that I've heard proficient skiers say they wish they could go back to being a beginner and fall down all over again. Whether they meant it or not is another thing altogether.

Skis will seem clumsy at first even though you will probably be started on shorter skis than your body weight and height actually require. Boots may also seem strange because they are so heavy and, of course, moving sideways is difficult with five feet of ski connected

to you. However, this is something you'll quickly get used to and you will soon learn the best ways of moving about when not actually skiing downhill.

One aspect that frightens most beginners is the gradients which they imagine they will begin on. Well it is very rare that you are expected to learn to ski on anything more than a five-degree slope, so flat in fact that you don't have to get on a lift to get to it. These very flat runs and the slightly steeper 'beginners' runs' are called blue runs and are usually marked in blue on ski maps and with blue poles on the piste itself. The next stage up from blue is the intermediate red run which is something for beginners to look forward to. You should reach the bottom rung of the intermediate standard by the end of your second week's skiing. The hardest runs are the black runs which present a challenge to advanced intermediates and will usually entertain the most advanced skiers. You can decide for yourself when you've reached advanced stage; I'm certainly not even though I've been skiing for some ten years.

A few resorts colour their blue runs green for some reason and some shade them half and half. You should also know that a black run in one resort may be very different in terms of difficulty from that in another. I skied down a black run in Italy during my second week of skiing and was awarded a three star gold medal – the highest the ski school has to offer. Now, I can't believe that that black run was much steeper than some of the blue ones I've skied in Switzerland and Austria. So you see that the criteria they use to differentiate between runs are very vague. Presenting me with a three star gold was ridiculous, though at least it gave me something to flash around at home! A friend who had been to another resort on his fourth week's skiing was awarded a two star bronze only, yet he is undoubtedly a better skier.

If You have Skied Before

Although this is not a 'learn to ski' book, it's important to remind you that one week of beginner's ski tuition does not mean you have learned to ski. It is vital to keep up lessons until you are a reasonably competent skier and after that it may be worth while taking the odd refresher lesson to make sure you haven't developed any bad habits. It is relatively easy to zoom down a mountainside as fast as you can but completely lacking in any style. If you are doing it wrongly and you continue to neglect your style, you will find that those who have taken their time and learned the right way can slide gracefully down the steep slopes at high speed while you're still stuck at the top.

Checking your Equipment

Before you start skiing (or rather falling over), it's very important to check that your equipment is fitted correctly. Boots should be tight fitting, but you should be able to move your toes! Most important is your binding, which on the one hand should be tight enough to hold your boot on to your ski throughout the normal stresses and strains of skiing (in other words it shouldn't come off when you make a tight turn), and on the other it must be loose enough to come off if you do have a tumble. The best test, therefore, is to pull up your bindings as hard as you can while leaning forward until they come out. You will need someone to stand on your ski while you're doing this, or obviously it will come up with your boot. The second test is to get someone to kick you in the foot; not a sensible suggestion in normal circumstances but if your boot doesn't give way, your bindings are too tight. You'll be able to tell if they're too loose because your boot will keep on falling off the ski without your doing anything remotely strenuous.

Exercise on Snow

After you've spent so long exercising at home (well haven't you), it would be a shame to spoil it all by not warming up properly when you're finally on the piste. If you're unlucky you will discover, particularly at the start of the season when the weather is most wintry and cold, that stiff muscles rupture the soonest. If you are in ski school you'll have to perform this warming-up ritual anyway.

The most useful exercises for skiing are those performed on skis. Hold a single ski pole at each end, raise your arms above your head and twist your entire body around to the left and right. Another exercise is called 'toe touch'. While still holding a ski pole at each end, touch your right foot with your left hand and left foot with your right hand (you'll find that you'll have to do this one at a time unless you've got a rubber ski pole or are some sort of contortionist). Knee bends are pretty essential for when you're doing those downhills; bend your legs as if in a sitting position but lean your upper body as far forward as possible still holding the ski pole but this time in the middle for balance rather than at each end.

There are plenty of other exercises involving swinging your arms, jumping up and down with your skis on, lifting one foot off the ground, bending sideways and so on. As long as you stretch as many of the muscles you use in skiing as possible, you can't really go wrong. I think the best thing I've ever done for muscle fitness is ballet – a new dimension for me in stretching. Although there is such a thing as 'ski ballet', it's not quite the same.

Ski school

From the moment that you first put on a pair of skis until you are at least at advanced intermediate standard, you will need a good deal of tuition to ensure that you learn to ski correctly. It is not too difficult to whizz precariously down a mountain and, through luck and natural balance, not fall over. But to go down the steeper slopes and to start feeling comfortable on skis, you need to learn how to ski properly.

Ski school classes begin at the very start of your holiday on the slopes and pupils are often divided into categories by a short test. If you're a complete beginner you just say so and you will start from scratch. Those of you that have been before, however, may be asked to give an example of your ability, such as skiing down a very gentle slope and making one turn. This is to show the instructors if you can do snow plough turns or are beginning to transfer your weight from one ski to another, or even if you're carving your turns properly.

The trouble is that if you've just put on a fresh pair of skis, after a year or so away from the slopes, you'll not only be very dubious about skiing straight off but also you'll probably be a little rusty on style. On top of that you'll be conscious of everyone else watching you and so you'll be as careful as possible not to fall over so as not to be relegated to the beginners' group. However, the ski instructors will allow for all this so you've nothing to worry about. In any case when the groups do get going, if you find yourself in a class either too advanced or too backward, you will be able to move up or down.

There are seldom more than ten people in each group and of course ski school is a great way to make friends. Different people react to the school in different ways; some people feel restricted by having to wait around for the entire class to take its turn or frustrated that the whole tuition period is being spent practising a few traverses when they want to get moving. Most people are embarrassed by the instructor staring up at them when they are the last to practise a manoeuvre and the rest of the school has already gone down.

You almost invariably feel that you are a burden to the others and this is why most instructors will pile on the praise if you do something right. It's also nice when members of each group compliment each other whenever possible, not necessarily when someone does

something right but just if they're making some noticeable improvement. But I'm making ski school sound like psychology cum stage début – in fact it's almost always an awful lot of fun and though most people take the learning seriously in a desire to improve their skiing, it is the pure enjoyment of all skiing which wins the day.

Ski school should be seen as a lesson on how to improve technique and it should rarely be used for practice. In other words you should have a lot of different ideas on technique drummed into you though you won't have much time to try them out in the lesson. For example, when you've moving up from basic parallel turns to advanced parallel turns, your instructor will probably tell you to keep your torso facing down the slope, to first put your weight on your outer ski, then plant your pole and ski down and, as you go into a turn, to transfer your weight and lift your body as you change direction. This helps you to carve turns and to develop a feeling of floating rather than skidding around corners. However, when you first do it you're more likely to experience a sensation of falling rather than floating as you'll never remember to do everything at once.

It is usually after ski lessons when you're practising on your own or with friends that everything will start going right. You'll feel pretty good because you're skiing correctly and movements that you had to think about before will just come naturally. Though the above example was for advanced intermediates, it's the same at all levels. So, don't worry if you can't do something right in the ski class, practise it when you're free skiing and impress your tutor with what you've learnt the next day. One word of warning, don't ski alone if it can be avoided, always go with a friend in case either of you should run into difficulties. However safe a piste or resort may seem it's always best to have someone you know around and a lot more fun too.

The ski school instructor

I should probably have told you before but it's not only important to fall over, it's important to fall over with style. You should always exaggerate falls, roll down as much mountain and kick up as much snow as possible. Only stop when you feel you've reached the most ridiculous position you can (it is a little known fact that certain national football squads spend winter breaks in the Alps, practising dives).

Actually though, it's not important to fall over well when you're with your ski instructor – just fall over. The best idea is to walk towards your tutor with arms outstretched as if in greeting and then fall over your skis. This will come naturally to you if you're wearing skis for the first time. It will also break the ice (awful) and not only lead to your being treated gently by the rest of the class but also to receiving the most comprehensive and intensive instruction from your ski teacher. If you start off badly you'll have plenty of room for improvement whereas those who try to impress their instructor can get only worse. If they're very unlucky they really will impress their instructor and get moved up to the next group where they'll be completely out of their depth. That's the theory of the instant fall ploy anyway. If it doesn't work that way it is, at least, one more good excuse.

Yet another is your instructor's vocabulary. That is whether or not he or she can speak English. Now all the brochures labour around in the belief that English-speaking instructors are greatly preferable to the foreigners when the opposite may well be true. Some companies are even introducing their own ski schools direct from Britain, but where does that leave you, the innocent punter out for a good time?

I'll give you an example, an attractive member of the opposite sex skis expertly past the faltering line of your ski school and beckons you to follow. In a foreign school you whizz off in pursuit of your new idol, and catch up with your ski school later, walking up to the bemused instructor, slapping him on the back and bellowing: 'Sorryo, Regio I – thought – you – wanted – us – to – go – to – the – bottom.' Now rather than make an issue of it, Regio, who'll not have understood anything you've said, will smile at your gestures of friendship and let you go straight back into the class. Now just try that with your English-speaking ski school, no chance! There's also no excuse for skiing awfully because you couldn't understand that 'Bender zee neez' meant 'Bend your knees'.

Another problem with the English-speaking tutors is that a lot of them are flown in from the United States and New Zealand. In itself that isn't a problem, but they seem to be covered by some perverse insurance scheme whereby if a member of their class is injured, they are responsible. Then you have to claim your insurance back through their insurance company or something equally ridiculous. Anyway that's the reason they gave us for not allowing us to do any free skiing (skiing out of classes) and why we weren't permitted to take the odd risk now and then. And by 'risk' I mean little things only like jumping over a bump or something.

So, what of the instructors themselves? Well there is a great variety as you may imagine: big ones; small ones; young ones; old ones; fat ones; thin ones; and so on! Sadly some of the younger and randier tutors do seem to act remarkably like couriers in their overtures towards the female members of their ski group. This basically means that there is a lot of 'touch' skiing with the hunky tutor helpfully guiding the shaky young girl's basic snow plough by sliding his skis in between hers'. Of course this blatant pass is fun for the girl if she is mutually attracted and extremely annoying if she's not, but it's also terribly irritating for the rest of the class who are left standing around while the tutor practises every manoeuvre individually with his star pupil.

However, a lot of these ski instructors aren't 'like that' at all; and you're less likely to get a useless instructor than you are a useless courier if you want to look at it that way. Many, if not most, take their job seriously and enjoy watching their classes improve under their instruction. Some are even so perfect that they don't show off how good they are to the rest of the class – but not many.

Ski guides

One of the major innovations in ski holidays of recent years has been the introduction of ski guides. The development of this profession since its introduction in less years than you can count on the fingers of one hand has been amazing. Most of the major holiday companies employ them, often in every resort, and urge you to ski with them. Nearly all such companies will state sternly, after a flowery introduction: 'Ski guides are not instructors and so are not for beginners or slow intermediates who need professional teaching. But for those who can keep up, only.'

This is quite sensible and honest advice to stop guides from being treated as ski instructors. However, on the occasions I have skied with them, and on certain promotional videos, they have been very helpful with advice on how to ski across certain types of terrain and in just providing tips on style. The idea of the ski guide, though, is to show the more experienced skiers around the resort. The ski guide, you see, will know all there is to know about skiing in a certain resort and can show you the best runs suited to your ability or a particularly interesting run. So they are very different from even the most advanced ski school classes.

Like ski school, you may well meet up with skiers of a similar ability to yours whom you'll be able to ski with again when you're not with your guide; very handy if you're on your own or have come on holiday with someone who can't ski nearly so well as you. Incidentally, don't be put off skiing with a novice, even if you're advanced standard, you may have the same pleasure as the ski tutor in seeing how they improve. It's also great fun seeing how much enjoyment they get out of learning, especially if you were the cause of their coming on a skiing holiday in the first place. You can't spend your whole holiday with them, however, 'the call of the piste' is bound to happen sooner or later and you'll be off! Never try to teach a novice yourself, however advanced your own standard. You won't know the ins and outs of basic technique unless you're a trained teacher. Therefore be helpful out of ski school but don't try to replace it.

Ski guides, like snow guarantees, are one of the major areas of competition between the tour operators. If you walk around the ski shows and meet the different operators (who will have a lot of ski guides on their stands), you'll find a great deal of disagreement as to who has the better ski guides. A common argument is: 'Well, although it says in the brochure that our guides aren't ski teachers, we make sure that all are trained to BASI level 3, 1984 standard.'

Frankly, I find all this bickering rather pointless, I'm sure all or most of the guides are quite capable of doing their jobs. If they're not, or the guides turn out to be couriers in a ski suit, the holidaymakers will work this out and the company will be blacklisted by them in future.

The ski lift

There seem to be a number of ski books on the market at present which give the impression that skiing is downhill all the way. Unfortunately this isn't the case and one of the ironies of skiing is that, in general, the better you become the more time you spend on the ski lift. This has given rise to a well-known skiers' saying (which I've just thought up) that proclaims: 'What comes down, must go up!'

There are two basic types of lift. There is the drag lift which pulls you up the slope while you keep your skis on the ground and there is the chair lift or cable car in which you sit or stand; they are suspended from a cable.

The Poma or Button Lift

Now as you need to use the lift more and more, the type of lift you'll use will change depending on how high or far you want to travel. After a few goes, riding the lifts will seem like child's play, as most of the little foreign brats will be only too pleased to demonstrate whilst you sprawl around on the ground on your first attempt. I can well remember my first ride on a ski lift, which at the time seemed not unlike St George meeting the Dragon, but in fact the lift was not more than 100 metres long and travelling at about half a mile an hour.

The lift in question was a 'button' drag lift or Poma, named after its inventor, the Frenchman Pomagalski, and it is one of the oldest kinds and the first type which most beginners will encounter. It comprises a round plastic disc (not unlike a Frisbee) connected to an elastic wire, which in turn is attached to the moving wire cable; it works on the simple principle that the disc is slipped between your legs and placed flat across your bottom, so that when the elasticated wire is fully extended, there is a gentle tug and you start moving uphill. At least that's the theory. When I made my first trip on a Poma lift there was a gentle tug, my legs went in opposite directions, I sat down to stop myself doing the splits and found myself being dragged uphill rather

painfully by a plastic disc which I was having difficulty in removing from between my legs!

However, don't be alarmed, my limbs are still intact as fortunately there is always a guard at both the top and bottom of the lift who can stop it at any time – which mine kindly did for me, and the safety bindings had released my skis anyway. So apart from being publicly humiliated in front of a large queue of expert Italian skiers who looked at me as if I was some sort of jelly-monster, my reputation and more importantly, my body, were unscathed.

My first mistake had been not to place my skis together and pointed uphill. When you are a beginner, you don't have proper control of your skis and so if your skis are pointing at anything other than straight ahead and in the direction that the lift is going or are not perfectly parallel your skis will invariably go in whatever direction they wish, you will not be able to stop them and you will fall over. You cannot snow plough up a mountain, you must rely on balance rather than on physical strength. So first of all, make sure your skis are *straight*.

My second mistake was to sit down (though having made the first mistake I had little choice); there is no bending of the neez involved in riding a drag lift, you should let the lift power be transmitted to your skis, so stand as straight as possible while still comfortable and relaxed. If you lean back on a drag lift, it will give way and you will fall over.

Although these two things are most important it is also essential, particularly if you are a first-timer, to concentrate on what you're doing all the way up the slope. Loss of concentration frequently leads to loss of balance and falling over halfway up is one of the worst things you can do. This is because if you're in front of some more beginners on the lift, they are likely to crash into you unless you can get out of the way in time, which though often funny can of course be dangerous and will make you unpopular. Secondly, if you fall onto an area off piste you may have a walk back to the main slope which can often be a pain. Thirdly, you will probably be part of a group which means either you have to wait for them or they have to wait for you (which is definitely not going to make you popular), and finally, of course, you've wasted all that time getting on the blasted thing in the first place.

Unfortunately, there are times when you may not be able to avoid falling off as unless the drags are well looked after which is rare, the track beneath them becomes deeply grooved by the many skiers passing over the same snow. You will normally have to follow these 'tram lines' but large bumps in the track may develop where many skiers have passed over areas of different snow types, which you may find difficult to ride at first. Hence you hit a bump, lose your balance and fall over. There's not a lot you can do about that until your standard improves, I'm afraid.

Now when you first get on a ski lift, providing the attendant knows you are a beginner, he will normally hold the 'seat' or 'Frisbee' part of the lift for you and even help you to sit on it (possibly the highlight of the holiday), but what happens when you've finally and heroically made it to the top and want to get off?

Well, you'll probably know when you are at the top because there's usually a few signs saying, 'You are at the top' in some foreign language. You will also notice a large bank of snow coming towards you and a big wheel that the drag wire goes round before descending again with your 'Frisbee'. Just before you hit the snow bank there should be a flat area and it is here that you jump off. Timing is essential, you must pull the 'Frisbee' and its handle on the elastic wire down between your legs, push it out in front of you and then let it go.

If you want to be really smart you can start pointing your skis away from the snow bank, and at a tangent to the direction of the lift. Then, holding the 'Frisbee' in your hands rather than between your legs, let it give you a little pull out of the way, before letting it go. On second thoughts though, perhaps it would be better to leave that stage until you've learnt how to get off properly. Two of the most frequent mistakes are to get off too soon and start going backwards downhill (and there is nothing much more alarming than that!) or to get off too late and end up careering feet first into the snowbank with two feet of ski holding you there.

Beginners are at a definite disadvantage when getting off drag lifts, because the only way they can get away from the top without falling over is to snow plough, and as the top has usually been flattened, they won't go very far in a snow plough position. This leads to many first-time skiers, having successfully got on and off the lift without incident, being stuck at the top with the next person about to run into the back of them. You will know if you are causing the obstruction because of the shouts of: 'Get out of the way you bloody idiot' coming towards you from below, and the sight of a red-faced lift attendant making strange grimaces, as well as the muttering sounds these foreigners are apt to make, in your general direction. So you must just get away from the top of the lift as well, and as quickly as you can, preferably without losing control. When the top of a lift does become congested the lift attendant will normally stop the lift while he yells to everyone standing around to move.

Like the bottom of the piste, the top of the lift is a communal area where friends meet up and then stand around contemplating the pleasure or terror the slopes hold in store. It is also a good place to watch other skiers, and as the beginners know they are going to fall over anyway, they usually hold back as long as possible. Therefore the tops of lifts are frequently crowded and often with many experienced skiers who can't be bothered to move out of the way; so set them an example.

Another problem with getting off a lift can be that there is not enough space to turn around; I remember in particular the top of one drag lift at Saas Grund, near Saas Fee in Switzerland, which allowed only about five feet of turning space. The lift was a T-bar which I shall deal with next; and though I was at intermediate standard I found it extremely difficult to jump off the lift without hitting the snowbank. Of course the experts can turn on a pin head, but there are few true experts, and that time the fault was with the design of the lift.

The T-bar

Next step up from the Poma lift is the T-bar. The lift is so named because yes, you've guessed it, it is shaped like a T, only upside down. You normally ride it in pairs, which makes it a sociable lift, but I think it is slightly easier to fall off it than a Poma lift. It works in exactly the same way as a Poma except that the two side pieces of the bar go across your bottom and that of your travelling companion.

I must say I absolutely hate the T-bar, possibly because of the experiences I had with it in Saas Grund. I find it difficult to counter my weight with the other person's, or to stand up straight, and it often turns into a fight between whoever I am with and me to stop the weight driving one or the other of us into the side of the track. On one memorable occasion I was halfway up the slope when my ski binding, which had come loose, got entangled with my friend's and my ski came off my boot. I managed to put it back on at once, but then it happened again and I fell sideways into a deep drift, just struggling up in time to see my friend disappearing over the rise with two skis on his right foot!

Riding a T-bar is more or less the same as riding a Poma lift, though, and you should try to relax as much as possible and let your natural balance pull you up effortlessly. The only problem you may encounter is getting off at the top, again especially when there is limited space. One person must hold the T-bar while the other skis off, and then let it go himself. Mix-ups invariably happen, particularly among the polite British who insist on saying 'After you . . .' 'Oh no, after you . . .' and so on, until they have hit the snowbank. The classic misadventure, however, is when the person sitting on the righthand side of the T-bar wants to ski off to the left, while the one on the left, of course, wants to ski to the right. Always good for a laugh!

You may sometimes have to catch a T-bar on your own, either because you are the only one there or your 'B.O.' is so bad that no one wants to ride with you. Obviously you have to make up for the fact that there is no one to counterbalance your weight and so you must lean a little to the right if you are sitting on the lefthand side of the T-bar. Whatever you do, though, don't try to put the T-bar between your legs like a Poma, the likely injury does not bear thinking about!

The Hand Pulley

I don't know the official name for this one, so I am using the descriptive term. Apart from special training equipment and minor variations, this is the last type of drag lift you are likely to come across. It is also the most basic and usually a temporary arrangement spanning 50 metres or less. It consists simply of a cable wire, with rubber handgrips at intervals, which moves around two powered wheels at the top and bottom of a very slight gradient. All you can say about it really is that when you grab a handgrip you risk having your arm pulled out of its socket because there is a sudden lurch as the rope pulls you forward.

However easily your skis slide, you cannot go from being stationary to travelling at say 5 mph, without some tug. From the start onwards the ride is a bit of a strain as you are pulling your entire body weight uphill with one arm. Still, at least it is easy to get off, you just let go.

The only other thing to say about drag lifts is that you should stay on the track that has been created. It is possible, you see, to swerve onto the soft snow at the side between the support posts, but such activity can occasionally lead to the wire coming off the wheels, leaving you unpopular and in trouble. More likely you will become so cocky you will forget what you are doing and crash into a support post or something, leaving you unconscious and unforgettable as the idiot on the drag lift!

Chair Lifts

Next up from the drag lift is the chair lift which can carry from one, two, three to even four people per chair. Chair lifts come in all shapes and sizes and are probably my favourite type of lift. They are extremely simple to use and, though perhaps a little more frightening than drag lifts in the first instance, they are a lot simpler to ride. Chair lifts will normally take you higher than a drag lift, drifting peacefully above the snow and pine trees – ahhh, wonderful!

To get into a chair lift, just line up in the marked position then when it comes round, sit down as you feel it come into contact with the back of your calves (most chairs have padding here so they don't bump your legs too much when they hit them). Make sure you don't sit down before you feel the chair touch your legs or you will not only look very silly but you might end up getting hit in the back of the head. Once you are seated the chair will quickly ascend and you should pull the foot support down from above you and rest your skis on that – then just enjoy a relaxing ride. Some chair lifts even incorporate blankets to put across your knees. Getting off the chair lift is also easy, you will see the gentle downward slope ahead of you as the chair descends, so lift your foot rest up, wait for your skis to hit the slope then just stand up and ski off.

The only real problem is once again largely for beginners, when not enough space or sufficient gradient is provided for getting off so you can't glide out of the chair's way quickly enough. Sometimes also there isn't enough space to move without falling over.

Tele-cabines

Used in the bigger resorts for carrying people from the very bottom to the top of the slopes and in some resorts for taking people up from the village or town to the bottom of the slopes. These cable cars will normally carry between two and six people, fully enclosed, with the skis inserted in racks on the roof. There is little to be said about them except that they are usually packed during the rush hours at the start and end of skiing, and though they hug the mountainside more closely than the giant cable cars (coming up next), the drop beneath can be vast and so these are one of the scariest modes of transport if you are slightly afraid of heights. The worst possible thing that can happen is when it is a windy day and your little tele-cabine is being blown about in the wind, the lift is switched off and you are left dangling in mid-air with nothing but a mile-long drop and surrounded by some extremely uncomfortable-looking people. But the danger is minimal, because tele-cabines are as safe as the other lifts which is very, very safe! (fingers crossed).

The Giant Cable Car

This is the biggest lift attached to a cable wire and it transports large numbers of people over long distances. This is the one you have seen in the James Bond movies and that has a pylon support only every 400 yards or so, which is the obstacle that creates the sensation I am now going to warn you about for your first trip. Because the large pylons are few and far apart the wire between them sags in large loops which means there is a sharp rise just before you reach the pylon. It also means the lift often tips forward and then back to a certain degree, not a lot but enough to notice, when you go over the pylon. This is just the way it is designed and does not mean you are about to plummet half a mile to your death, though I for one wouldn't blame you for thinking that. It is funny because you don't feel so 'threatened' in a lift full of a hundred sweaty skiers as you do when you are in a little tele-cabine. This is despite the fact that you will be swaying around much higher up and with less frequent, though equally strong, support.

Besides these lifts there are mountain railways and buses in some resorts and, in Saas Fee at least, they are currently spending a considerable sum building an underground skiers' railway which will whizz up through the heart of the mountain. And for the richer skier, heli-skiing is available in most resorts.

Lifts are a very sociable place for skiers, equalled only perhaps by the ski school. Standing next to someone on a T-bar you feel you have to start some sort of conversation, and you can have a lot of fun trying to understand each other, assuming your partner is not English. It is the same to some extent with the ski school.

The thing that amazes me most about ski lifts is how they get some of them up there. I know they must be built in the fairer months, but there is one in Zermatt, for example, which is carved through a jagged rock peak hundreds of feet up. So high in fact that it is above the glacier which is there all year round. It certainly says something for human ingenuity and how far people are prepared to go to expand skiing areas.

Note

Unfortunately, before getting on a lift you will normally find you have to queue. Even more unfortunately, the Brits are the only people who know the meaning of the word. It is therefore important that you quickly learn the art of teaching foreigners how to queue. By far the most effective method of doing this is to help them test their safety bindings by pushing your ski stick down on the rear release lever when they try to push past. Indeed, the main purpose of ski sticks is for controlling queues and retaining your own position. Make sure you are bigger than the other skier though, or make sure you are in a suitably, 'anti-pushing-in foreigners' queue that will back you up in the more extreme cases where physical violence comes into play.

Your manners on skis

As I pointed out earlier in this book, there are a number of different categories of skier that you are likely to come across on the slopes. Unfortunately some of these are not only idiots but frequently selfish and bad mannered, so it is up to you to maintain a sense of fair play on the slopes. Most of the 'rules' surrounding skiing are just common sense and are very similar to the Highway Code. Just like with cars, people are only tempted to go faster as equipment and its safety aspects are constantly improved and the conditions of the piste get better. Youngsters in particular are prone to losing control of their skis at speed and another growing cause of accidents (and one of the most lethal) is the high-speed collisions between skiers.

The rules themselves are very brief and are really just good, plain sense:

Rule one	When starting off, look uphill for skiers coming down. Don't pull out without looking
Rule two	When overtaking skiers in front of you, you are responsible. Try to let the skier know you're coming down and on which side you intend to pass him – in general just be careful and be ready for any sudden turns from the skier in front of you
Rule three	The converse of rule number two, look behind you before making a sudden turn because there is bound to be some idiot not adhering to rule two and about to run into you
Rule four	Always give way to oncoming traffic
Rule five	Do not ski between ski schools and their instructors, try to pass on the right where possible
Rule six	Get away from the top of the lift as soon as you can (see the lifts section)
Rule seven	When you do stop, rest at the sides of the pistes
Rule eight	Always try to ski with or near a companion, especially in less than perfect conditions, and stick to the marked pistes unless you are with a guide

Rule nine	In the lift queue wait your turn, if anyone tries to push in it is legitimate practice to thump them with a ski pole and other people queuing will normally help you out here. Don't try it with the officials or the ski instructor though!
Rule ten	Don't mess around in any way when you are on the lifts – ride them properly
Rule eleven	When you're putting on your skis, don't give them the chance of sliding downhill and hitting someone in the back like in *The Omen* or something. Always fit them on the flat
Rule twelve	When leaving the pistes at the end of the day, do not ski down the road back to your hotel but carry your skis. Carry them over your shoulders with the tips facing downwards in front of you. And don't swing them round horizontally when you turn thus decapitating 15 innocent skiers

Many of these rules are law in alpine resorts, as well as good sense and good manners, so try to stick to them – they won't interfere with your enjoyment. Besides I'd far rather meet you in the restaurant than in the hospital.

Emergencies

Don't worry about avalanches for, provided you don't ski where you're not supposed to, you're more likely to be killed crossing the road outside your hotel. Ski centre staff are largely responsible for maintaining the general safety of each resort and restricting skiing to safe areas.

However, smaller accidents do happen and it's no good hoping that you'll never be the one or that your assistance won't be needed to help a fellow skier. Most resorts have stretcher sleighs situated at convenient points such as the tops and bottoms of ski lifts so you can always alert the ski lift operators. Helicopter recovery is also operated by telephoning from ski lift stations and so on. In the meantime make your patient as warm and comfortable as possible and cross a pair of skis in the snow above them as the international symbol of accident.

The only bad news for those on death's door is that in certain places (or so it is rumoured), stretcher parties won't come out until they've been paid. And you thought it was the skier who was sick!

People you'll meet on the slopes

The 'I Think I'm Franz Klammer' or Kamikaze Skier

Just as you have managed to regain your balance after a particularly shaky start on that wobbly second day, you will be totally 'burned off' by one of these pretentious speed fanatics. Paying no heed to blind bends or to the screams of women and children except as encouragement, they bomb past, running over the fronts and tails of your skis as if you were a slalom post and spraying you with snow as they do a right turn.

However, this type of skier does serve a useful purpose for not only does he inspire you to become good enough to chase after him and gain your revenge when he has to stop in order to push into the lift queue at the bottom but he also causes the greatest amount of amusement when he falls over (tee hee).

There is no danger from the real racing skiers on most pistes because however lethal they look, they are totally in control and could turn on a milk bottle top (still a good laugh when they fall over though)! The kamikaze skiers are not nearly so safe and are frequently downright dangerous, so are best avoided at all costs.

The 'Oh my God I'm Going to Fall over' Skier

Used as slalom posts by the kamikaze skiers, these people have entirely the wrong attitude. They are so worried about the possibility of falling over that they do so because they are so nervous!

Such people cause difficulties for even the most conscientious skiers when let loose on the main pistes and they should remain on the nursery slopes a while longer. It's always off-putting to come skiing down only to find an assault course of out-of-control and crashing learners blocking the last bit. If you're particularly unlucky, you'll also meet them on the drag lift after they've fallen off and stopped that. Going past them will only break their concentration, cause them to fall and one fall always leads to another. You have to wait until they're all on the floor before you can get past.

The real problem for skiers is when the fear of falling persists past learner stage as it makes any progress in ability far slower.

The 'That wasn't my Fault' Skier

The egocentric, 'I'm a professional skier' who refuses to admit that he can make a mistake and blames all mishaps on his equipment or on some other unlikely cause (such as someone else). It's always clear to everyone that he's just lost his balance or his control. Typical excuses include:

'I wouldn't have fallen but that person who cut me up at the top of the slope ruined my concentration.'

'I was going fine until that person on the third chairlift across the valley screamed something offensive about the Queen.'

'Phew, I never expected the drop to be that steep over the hill, I was allowing for ten degrees less gradient.'

And so they go on and on . . .

Of course, things do go wrong because of loose skis and people skiing without regard for anyone other than themselves, but making up far-fetched excuses every single time that you have an accident does nothing but make you the butt of a lot of jokes. Examples are: 'I was doing great until that tree swerved out in front of me' or 'All right, who built the brick wall in the middle of John's piste?'

The Perfect Two-year-old Foreign Skier

One of the greatest ego deflators must be when you're bursting with pride after skiing what you believe to be a beautiful run and two brightly-coloured little foreign kids come hurtling past you – one going between your legs and the other somersaulting over your head – turning you from a good skier into a wally without saying a word.

Even more embarrassing is when you fall over, particularly while getting on the drag lift, and they turn to look condescendingly at you as they do their acrobatics on their way up the slopes. The awful thing about the little darlings is that they seem incapable of falling over; they can go straight down the blackest ski run doing their little snow ploughs and looking back over their shoulders to blow bubbles at you but still they do not fall. It must be something to do with a low centre of gravity or something. And the poor British children in the kindergarten are completely outclassed. They hate the cold wet snow and are sometimes heard saying: 'want to go home Mummy.'

The only possible consolation is that while you dance, drink and

make merry in the early hours, the two-year-old foreign skiers will have been sent to bed hours before. But that won't seem such a happy memory next morning when they're running round screaming and full of energy while your head tries to bang your ears together.

What makes it all worth while though is when the impossible happens and one of them falls over, particularly while doing their antics on the drag lift – what bliss!

The Beautiful People

Also the rich and living-by Palm Beach people. These are the children of the fat Americans with the codpiece-like cameras that strut around the 'cute' little village wearing caps with 'Major General Sir John "Big Boy" Washington Texas Junior, Vietnam, Korea and most of World War II' written on them and loads of medals pinned to their regulation army T-shirts.

Their beautiful children are the ones that call everyone 'you guys', ski beautifully and look immaculate even after the most horrendous blizzard. Still their ex-army parents aren't a lot better – or worse depending on which way you see these things – they let their little darlings persuade them into an afternoon's skiing during which they tank down the slopes at enormous speed looking so professional that the bumps are miraculously ironed out so that there is no chance of them falling over and sadly they never do. In the evenings the beautiful people may be found dining on the terraces of the most expensive restaurants in town overlooking the main street.

The Fantasy Skier

Also contains elements of the 'Kamikaze' or 'That wasn't my fault' Skier. Not content with skiing for pleasure the Fantasy Skier creates Winter Olympics in his mind to win and turns moguls into 200-metre world record-breaking ski jumps. When he hits a tree, the offending plant grew itself there while he wasn't looking and it is not uncommon for brick walls to build themselves into his imagination. Except when the Fantasy Skier is a beginner playing at being Franz Klammer, he is relatively harmless. If you pass someone muttering to themselves don't worry about it; it may be the first sign of madness but it's worth it to the Fantasy Skier.

The True Professional Posing Skier

This is the young lady who comes down backwards, on one ski, reading a copy of *War and Peace* and singing the Swiss National Anthem to herself. Well worth watching, as are all professionals who really know what they're doing and do it unbelievably well.

The American Skier

Usually buys lift passes by the day as this is the most expensive way. Calls everyone 'guys' and skis better than most as they do little else. American skiers are normally a combination of the Fantasy, Beautiful People and 'I think I'm Franz Klammer' skiers and are best avoided. In fact they are really the 'I think I'm Ben Johnson' skiers, Ben Johnson being the golden boy with the three-mile mouth who won the men's downhill in the last Winter Olympics – and they'll not let us forget it!

Avoiding starvation in the resort

Although you may see yourself as a pleasant addition to the mountain scenery, the people who live all year long in your resort will probably see you as a necessary intrusion to be put up with. You are a tourist first, and a skier second, and as a tourist you are fresh meat for the vultures that run almost every business in your resort.

However 'picturesque and unspoiled' your brochure describes your resort, and however 'friendly and welcoming' Hans and Ethel Schmidt are in your secluded pension, you are still going to be ripped off left, right and centre. You are in a tourist resort, and they are the same all over the world (look at London). If it was not a tourist resort then you would not be going there with that huge travel company. Resorts vary from specially-built towns such as Les Arcs and part-time tourist resorts in Switzerland, Spain and Austria, to resorts that may once have been 'picturesque and unspoiled' villages but are now thoroughly commercial such as Zermatt.

Unfortunately there is no way you are going to avoid spending money, even getting killed in an avalanche will be expensive, but there is a way of not spending too much which simply involves following a few basic rules:

- Never buy anything at a mountain restaurant
- Never buy anything at a main street hotel or restaurant

■ Buy sun cream, films for the camera and so on before you go
■ Never buy a drink in a disco that was free to get into
■ Never have your film developed in the resort
■ Never go to a cheap restaurant recommended by any one other than a fellow tourist (everyone else is on commission)
■ Only get drunk on wine, in fact only drink wine – never the 'potent local brew ho ho ho', which you will find has a far more potent price than alcohol content
■ Only buy wine from the supermarket (or equivalent) – if possible buy all your food at the supermarket

The smart self-caterers will start planning the food intake before departure and if possible carry as much edible produce with them as possible – particularly things like spreads, biscuits, chocolate and stuff like that (incidentally, this is easier to do on coach trips as there are usually no restrictions on baggage weight). Then, if you buy some bread in the resort and prepare some sandwiches, they will make a very satisfactory lunch or perhaps tide you over for one evening. At virtually all resorts it is perfectly safe to take a drink and biscuits, chocolate and sandwiches with you up the slopes, and simply leave them near the lift station at the bottom of the slopes, so that you are able to eat, drink and make merry at lunch-time without breaking your back carrying the money required to buy a small Coke at the mountain restaurant.

I have been leaving food lying around ever since the first day I skied and I have yet to encounter a problem. However, remember to be sociable and dispose of all rubbish after you have eaten – I have yet to see a litter-strewn mountain and I hope I never will! Also, to be on the safe side, never leave anything particularly valuable, such as a nice flask, at the top; my lunch packs are pretty thrifty and a litre of water, a packet of biscuits and some sandwiches, worth about 50p in all, is all I take and so not really worth stealing in any case!

The evening meal is a different proposition and depends to a large extent on where you stay. The small 'unspoilt' Austrian and Swiss villages will certainly spoil your appetite with their prices, so it is largely a matter of shopping around. In Mayrhofen, a very popular beginners' and intermediates' resort, the food prices seemed generally high but there were at least two cosy little cafés which served large wholesome meals of a high standard at reasonable prices. Large meals are what you want after a hard day on the slopes, dainty meals are useless – however tasty and however little they are priced. They included high quality fish and chips, lasagne or spaghetti at prices around £2 to £3. Unfortunately other resorts such as Zermatt in Switzerland, a very up-market and artificial place, offers nothing below £4 for the foulest-tasting burger made out of some poor beast you don't wish to imagine. The problem with these places is that they are so secluded you can't escape from them, and the whole resort unites in its efforts to relieve you of as much money as possible during your stay.

The French ski stations, specially-built for the skier, offer the right sort of food, though as would be expected, the restaurants and even the supermarkets are rather on the costly side. Possibly the best place for cheap eating is Italy, where you can scoff yourself silly on spaghetti, pasta, lasagne, cannelloni, ravioli and a lot of other forms of pasta for only, say L40,000 per week. Oh, in case you have forgotten Italians often use the sterling pound sign to denote their own lira currency – 40,000 lira is now about £15. It is a nasty shock seeing your first £1000 cup of tea though!

As far as liquid intake is concerned, prices are generally quite stable and many alcoholic drinks are a lot cheaper than in Britain. Plus, of course, you can drink when you are thirsty rather than due to a certain phase of the moon or whatever it is that controls opening hours in Britain.

You will not, however, find pubs, only bars serving wine or lager in bottles and occasionally what the Continentals call beer, on draught too. You buy these in half or quarter litre sizes which are generally around one-third more than the price of the British pint or half-pint equivalents. However, the beer you are drinking – that is continental lager – would cost you at least as much in a British pub if you were crazy enough to wish to choose it above one of our own great brews! I'm also basing my estimates on prices in the north where I come from as in the south prices are often a third more.

It should be made clear though, that it is not so much what you drink as where you drink it. The bars, which are usually part of a shop or a hotel, are almost always smaller than pubs, with little atmosphere and a large quantity of foreign people in them. If you go into a posh hotel you are going to pay a lot more for the same drink served in a fancy glass, than you would in the bar at the back of the village sweet shop. But by far the worst is the 'free' disco where you hand the bartender £5 for an orange juice, lemonade and bottle of beer and make the mistake of complaining when you only get 50p change. You will then find there is a standard price of £1.50 per drink – be it a tonic water or whisky (£3 for both in the same glass!).

Bar prices for wine are very different from supermarket prices too, wine can often be bought for £1 a bottle abroad which, if it ever happens over here, will make home brew and possibly even British beer, obsolete. But in the bar you will pay at least that much for just one glass. Bottles of spirits such as rum and vodka are also sometimes a quarter of the price in Britain and certainly a lot cheaper than the so-called 'duty free', but in the bars the prices are not much different from back home. So private parties are a good idea if you are in the right accommodation, otherwise you will just have to make friends with someone who is!

One final thing on food, drink and prices. From time to time newspapers and magazines publish resort consumer price guides, the best of which give you the standard resort prices and the worst, 'the price of a cup of coffee in Italy is . . .', and then give you the English equivalent. These really are not worth the paper they are written on and are only of any use if they tell you the rate of exchange. Prices vary tremendously wherever you are, and it is up to you to look round for the best deals. The only guides worth seeing are to be found in some ski brochures giving lists of prices at the main supermarket in a particular resort at a specific time – these at least give you some idea of what you are going to have to pay; usually add on another 10 per cent.

The Mountain Restaurant

After a hard morning of bending zee neez, planting your poles and bumping your bottom, there is nothing like the mountain restaurant for collapsing in for the better part of an hour. It's these magnificent establishments that await the weary skier at the bottom of the piste with outstretched arms and over-priced cuisine.

Mountain restaurants vary greatly from large, open-plan designs that are very similar to mountaintop school dining halls to the more desirable little shacks and wooden or stone restaurants where a more cosy gathering is possible. The restaurants are very social places full of people discussing the day's best runs, most memorable falls and so on. Prices differ from restaurant to restaurant and from resort to resort though they are generally high. A plate of chips and a beer in a typical restaurant will cost you the equivalent of just under £2.

It's usually the more traditional restaurants that serve the best food . . . at a price. Typical dishes are stew, goulash, soup, pizza and the local variety of cake; while the drinks are coffee, hot chocolate and often mulled wine – stronger drinks warmed in temperature and potency – and hot fruit juices. The emphasis is on filling you up and keeping you warm. However, don't overdo it if you intend to do some strenuous skiing within an hour or two of lunch, especially if you've drunk some Glühwein or the equivalent.

It is the more subtle skier that uses the mountain restaurant to his or her advantage. First of all, they go to the lavatory, pretending that they're about to spend their life savings and buy a drink. But after coming out of the loo they make a dash for the door and then stand out on the terrace admiring the mountain scenery, relaxing and eating the chocolate and biscuits they brought up with them.

Mountain restaurants' rules and regulations differ considerably. Some will not allow you to eat your own packed lunches there, some will let you if you pay a small charge, and others don't mind at all. Many have outside terraces which are often the best part and there is rarely any objection to your eating your home-made lunch there.

It always amazes me just how they manage to build the restaurants so high. It is while you are 'cooling down' on the terrace that you can admire the beauty of the surrounding mountains. For me it's also a time to reflect on the grandeur and awesomeness of nature – I wouldn't stand much chance up alone in some of those forbidding peaks.

The courier

Well by now you should have had a chance to make up your mind about the courier. Was your first impression correct? Many people take couriers for granted and dismiss them as either good or bad, but perhaps it is worth looking at the job from a wider perspective. The courier has a very difficult job and with often a hundred or more people to look after, the variety and number of problems that arise are positively impossible to deal with. Imagine, for example, one hotel resident holding all-night parties in the room next to someone who is desperate to get to sleep so that he can be an early morning piste basher. There is little chance of the courier being able to change their rooms so he either has to tell the former to keep the noise down or the latter to stop complaining. In either event he will have one, if not two, dissatisfied customers.

Again it is the courier who must cushion the blow when you discover that most of the brochure's spiel about your accommodation and resort is wildly exaggerated. The courier, as the company's representative in the resort, is in the firing line and is usually the one that gets hit. Unfortunately, though, not even these good reasons in the defence of couriers are enough to excuse some of them. Not only are they sometimes undertrained but some are determined to have at least as much fun as the holiday-makers which means that they are not taking their job very seriously. This is the sort of courier who will latch onto the prettiest newcomer and smother her with attention while forgetting all about everyone else. Some couriers are keen skiers looking for cheap, all-season skiing and, knowing this and having no shortage of applications, the companies frequently underpay their couriers. To supplement their meagre incomes, some couriers may strike deals with the locals in return for recommending certain restaurants and so on.

So there is a clear distinction between those couriers who are efficient and know their job, which usually entails an intricate knowledge of their resort and company, and those that don't. It's very much 'pot luck' and there is no relationship, for example, between the size of the company and the standard of the courier. So whether your courier is a good one or not will probably depend on what sort of person he is regardless of the fact that his job is making sure that nothing goes wrong with your holiday in the resort.

Warming down

How far has all that pre-ski exercise got you, all those months of limbering up before you'd even set eyes on a mountain? Well, sadly, perhaps not as far as you may have hoped. Unfortunately there is no perfect exercise programme that simulates skiing movements absolutely, so even the very fittest may suffer the odd ache or pain for the first day or two. Half an hour of exercise cannot prepare you for six or eight hours of hard skiing (or hard falling over in the beginner's case).

You should, of course, avoid overdoing it on those first couple of days to give your body time to adjust but try remembering that when you're back on skis for the first time in a year and know that you have only six days to make the most of it – all common sense goes out of the window. It's useless preaching restraint, but if you do want to avoid sore muscles at the end of the day, you should stick to the gentler slopes for a few hours only in the early days and then build up gradually. This gives your muscles time to accustom themselves to the

rigorousness of skiing, but as I said, with six days of skiing it's hardly worth bothering them with the effort is it?

One of the commonest forms of *après ski* soreness is tension. The reason for this is simple, when you're skiing you are constantly alert and on the look-out for the unexpected, concentrating hard on the terrain and improving your technique as well as trying to avoid the piste bashers. Tension can often develop from the shoulders, as the result of constant contraction of the muscles, and it can frequently affect the neck and arms and also the legs in the less fit. There are a number of 'warming down' exercises that you can do to combat this tension. These include the old neck bend: simply stand up straight, with your arms at your sides, and move your head sideways from one shoulder to the other several times. Do not move your shoulders up towards your head but feel your muscles being strained on the stretched side of your neck. Don't strain them too much though! A variation is to stand on tiptoes and raise your arms up towards the ceiling, but that's a little more strenuous.

The shoulder shrug, another good and gentle relaxation exercise, involves lifting your shoulders up towards your ears and holding them there for a few seconds. Then drop your shoulders and move them round and round in circles while standing up straight all the time.

The hand push is a natural stretching exercise for many people. Interlock your fingers so that they overlap the backs of your hands, then turn your palms outwards and push your hands out in front of you as far as possible. If this doesn't stretch your shoulders, nothing will!

You should repeat these basic exercises whenever you have a spare moment, such as after skiing, before bed, and in the lift queue, and fix them so much in your mind that you even do them in your sleep! But talking of having things on your mind, you can avoid a good part of the strain and tension by adopting the correct mental attitude. Try and be as relaxed as possible when skiing; this not only reduces the tension that fear and concentration cause but also the chances of injury and even of falling.

It is very important not to just put your skis on, bash yourself about for a day and then gorge yourself at the restaurant, have a heavy drinking session, go to bed and then get back into the boots. You must give your body a chance to adjust to your new lifestyle, so warming down is a must.

AFTER SKIING

Après Ski

It is difficult to say precisely at what point skiing ends for the day and the evening begins; it is also difficult to explain exactly what *après ski* means. Well the answer all depends on who you are. The fanatical skiers, for example, do not believe in *après skiing*. For them there is only skiing, exercising and eating (plus a few trips to the lavatory for those not yet perfectly attuned). Then again there is the opposite type, the usually wealthy, full-time *après skier* who has been known to ski for as little as one or two days only during a week's winter sports holiday. Mr and Ms Average Skier, though, settle for standard *après ski* hours, which start after dinner and end when they fall asleep

(which may be only a few hours before skiing is due to start the next morning, according to circumstances).

So, what is *après ski*? Well technically, it is doing all the other traditional ski things like sitting around big log fires, listening to geriatric Austrians playing squeeze boxes or blowing enormous horns down your ear, eating cheese fondues and drinking Glühwein. Realistically, however, most people settle for a few drinks in the bar, followed by a few more drinks, a bop in the disco and then going back to consume any drink remaining in someone's room. While that'll do for a few nights, the organized *après ski* is worth trying if you can be selective. For example, the sledging evening is normally one not to be missed, but more of that later.

Probably the most important element of *après ski* these days is the *après ski* boot. These you should leave in the boot room so that you can change back into them instantly when depositing your skis and boots there at the end of the day. For the past few years now the main *après ski* boot has been the 'moon boot', a sort of padded wellington boot, which gives a firm grip on slippery surfaces. Before the moon boot the trendy *après skier* could be found wearing boots covered in goats' hair which looked remarkably like sawn-off, hollowed-out mammoth's feet. The problem with both types of boot is that they are extremely hot once you are indoors. They are great for roaming

around the resort; but when you are walking into a sweaty disco, the temperature change inside your boots, or rather the lack of it, can be quite disconcerting. For that reason the super new style of *après ski* boot has arrived, half the size, and yes, you've guessed it, twice the price!

So now you have your boots on, and preferably some nice colourful *après ski* wear (originality is better than high fashion), where do you go? How about Andorra? In this duty-free resort *après ski* is at its very cheapest with brandy or rum for less than 40p a measure. Italy is also one of the better nations for the alcoholic economisers. All through the Alps, fondues will be rammed down your throat. Only in Italy can you escape them by eating more than the average amount of pizza.

The evening for most, however, begins quietly. Having staggered back to your hotel or apartment, feeling as if you are floating on air without your skis and ski boots weighing you down, it is the time to collapse. It is now that the happy exertions of the day are finally felt and everyone flops on the bed, hopefully all on the same one, then some will fall asleep while others will manage to pull off the sticky ski wear first and drape it over the radiator before crawling into the shower. It is here that the difference between skiers really comes to the fore. Club 18–30 *après skiers*, for example, may well do things together and in a different order. They may remove their ski wear quickly, throwing it on the ground; jump onto the bed and then go into the shower. Others prefer a more leisurely pace. But there is certainly a period of relaxation prior to the evening meal.

For those in hotels the evening meal is, naturally, a regulated event. But for those on a self-catering holiday, it is the evening meal that can form the basis of the entire night's entertainment. Before eating there is the preparation of the meal which everyone must join in with and for the larger groups this means disaster. Then there is the meal out when the richer skiers can go to the nicest-looking restaurant they see and eat and drink far into the night. The more poverty-stricken skiers can walk round far into the night looking for the cheapest eating establishment in the resort and finally arrive just before closing time. Chalet parties are something else, of course, and the guests here may not ever need to leave their seats as the meals and the drinks roll one after another from the kitchens and the bars, carried by the trusty chalet girls. *Après ski* is very much a 'group experience' and that can be wonderful – unless you hate the rest of the group, in which case you are really stuck.

So, what of organized *après ski*? Well this varies considerably according to company and resort. It also differs from country to country. Although the modern French resorts have discotheques, bowling alleys and cinemas, they tend to lack the traditional 'community' events that you will find in Austria and Switzerland. For that reason the tour operators put a far greater emphasis on the provision of *après ski* in France than in most other countries. Obviously though, the amount of *après ski* provided by the operator depends on the individual resort.

Some of the organized *après ski* at the French ski station may include a film night, cheap disco night, special ice-skating night ('let's pretend we can play ice hockey and belt a few wops' is always a firm favourite with the fun-seeking Brits). There is also often a 'torchlight descent' in which you imagine you are skiing down beautifully just like in the films. This will often be after a special meal at the mountain restaurant, and in France there are many such meal-centred evenings, which usually deteriorate into wine-centred ones.

The best time of the year for the *après skier* is of course Christmas and New Year, when there should be a good Christmas dinner. Unfortunately the French eat their special dinner on New Year's Eve, and though you may have to pay around £10 for a good Christmas lunch, you will have to pay perhaps twice that on New Year's Eve. Christmas pudding lovers should note that the French idea of this marvellous mixture is not exactly the same as our own.

For the more energetic, who have preferably waited until some time after their Christmas dinner has gone down, there is the ancient French sport of 'poubelle racing', which involves jumping into a large plastic bag and throwing yourself down the piste. If your courier tries to tell you this is called sledging it is your duty to correct his pronunciation (see also page 103). The 'poubelle racing', and/or sledging, will normally follow a few drinks which will help you to relax thus lessening your chances of injury. Unfortunately your usual caution concerning gradients, slopes and speeds may also be affected. Sometimes the sledging style activities are dropped from the *après ski* schedules because of the number of injuries.

Après ski activities are usually posted up on the notice board in the entrance hall of your hotel or apartment. You will be told all about them at the good old welcome party, when everyone tries to be friendly and is helped on their way by the odd drink of free wine. These are well worth gate crashing whenever a new party arrives as the courier is so busy being friendly to everyone that he or she won't notice you have been to the past six such welcome parties.

There is, of course, no reason why you should not organize your own *après ski* activities. My own club has a far more exciting and varied programme than most tour operators are able to manage. Sadly, most of these schemes are far too dubious to mention in such a wholesome publication as this, but one example is the 'Save As You Fail Fund', where set fines (equivalent to about 25p usually) are levied on members for committing such crimes as: falling off the drag lift; being last down to breakfast; being first off the piste in the evening; and not wearing a tie to dinner (and on New Year's Eve wearing anything other than a tie for dinner!). At the end of the week the fund is quite high and we blow it all on the last night out. And of course disorganized snowball fights are a must from the moment you step off the coach in resorts.

In short, *après ski* is what you make it, and though some organized events are not to be missed, you should be able to create your own entertainment without too much taxing of the imagination!

Other sports you may care to try

Most of the holiday brochures happily rattle off a long list of the 'alternative winter sports' available in their resorts. But for those of us not imbued with the desire to watch some of the more obscure sports programmes on TV or to read widely on this particular subject, there is a big difference between what we're told we can and what it is we understand we can do! So here is a brief rundown:

Bandy, Shinty or Ice Hurling

One of those that you probably won't come across and somewhere between football and ice hockey. The latter has more or less superceded it. Bandy was included in the 1952 Winter Olympics but as each team lost one and won one, it was decided too boring to be included again – that's a guess incidentally. In rules it is similar to football and in violence it is similar to ice hockey.

Barrel Jumping

Again you probably won't find this one in many, if any, brochures. It involves wearing ice skates (I won't bother you with that one, we all know about Torvill and Dean), and jumping over a lot of barrels, at least 16 at once if you're interested in becoming world champion. Not commonly available but I'm sure that for a reasonable fee, some local will be more than willing to put you on the river with some old barrels.

Curling

You're likely to find this one in the brochures and it isn't too expensive or time consuming. Curling is one of the few winter sports in which the thrill of speed and danger is not the prime pleasure for it is the ice world's equivalent to bowls and the fun is in the competition. The game largely developed in Scotland over the last few centuries, so even if you lose you can claim that it's not the winning that's important but being smart enough to think the game up in the first place!

Hang Gliding

Perhaps the posy brochure's favourite picture is of someone hang gliding high above a mountainside with a pair of skis dangling from their feet. Well, this is a sport available to the casual skier and is certainly worth a try if you want to part with a large quantity of money (£30+) for a quick thrill (one trip). Hang gliding in ski resorts does not involve learning the sport but merely jumping off the mountainside with someone who knows what they're doing and by that I mean someone who knows how to hang glide, not how to make a lot of money quickly. So for one payment, you get one trip to tell your friends back home about. You can decide afterwards whether you think it is worth it!

Ice Golf

After a hard day on the piste what could be nicer than relaxing in the pool with a gentle game of golf? Yes, golf on a frozen lake is available in St Moritz but make sure you go before the thaw sets in around March time.

Langlauf

Cross-country skiing on the long thin skis you will see for sale in all the sportswear shops. Cross-country skiing is, obviously, skiing across flat land as well as up- and downhill.

Mono Skiing

Very similar to, if not the same as, snurf (see below), as you're skiing on one double-width ski instead of two normal skis. It's not too difficult for those who in any case look like they're skiing on one ski but for the rest of us . . . well.

Skidoo

The skier's motorbike. These mini bikes have miniature caterpillar tracks at the back and a single mini-ski at the front rather than a wheel to steer. As seen in some James Bond films, the good old all-conditions tricycle, with wheels like space hoppers, is available in some resorts as well.

Ski Music and Dream Lessons

Another gimmick in the trendy resorts, it's available if you think you can ski better with a cassette recorder blasting into your ears. Probably cheaper to take your own though.

Sledging

This is pretty well known to everyone but beware of exactly what the holiday companies mean by sledging. An evening's sledging, or 'toboggan evening' is often included in the *après ski* schedule, but one of the companies I travelled with thought that a toboggan was a black plastic bin liner! Still at least it was free, unlike the £5 we were charged the following year for a few hours on a piece of curved wood. In fact, throwing yourself down a hillside in pitch darkness wearing a bin liner was a lot of fun and helped to re-establish the British reputation of being 'seelee'. Bobsledding is very occasionally available, but you need instruction and this costs time and money and is more of an alternative to rather than a supplement to a ski holiday. 'Taxi ride' bobsleigh runs are sometimes available on a similar time/price basis as 'taxi ride' hang gliding – that is, at least £30 for 2 minutes.

Snow Shoe Walking

Can you guess?

Snurf

Great fun this one! A cross between skiing and surfing, or perhaps more between sledging and surfing, as you surf on the powder snow. Available in the trendier resorts such as Meribel and well worth a try.

Summer skiing

As the number of skiers increases, resorts often run out of time to fit them all in during the time the snow falls. For that reason some resorts have extended the season to 12 months of the year. Of course it isn't quite that easy, though many resorts manage to keep going through the year by inviting busloads of pensioners to come and admire the summer scenery, which is certainly worth doing even if you aren't a pensioner. Few resorts can boast permanent skiable snow and those that do are normally near a glacier where snow has been around for a few million years and isn't likely to pop off suddenly. The resorts themselves aren't usually so high as the glaciers and are bathed in mountain sunshine and greenery; but when you travel up a few thousand feet, by a series of lifts, you're back in the world of snow and ice.

You should start skiing as soon as possible after dawn, usually between 6 and 8 a.m. Depending on which direction the valley faces, the sun may reach you before it gets to the top so you can race it to the

top. Otherwise the sun may get to the mountain first giving you a nice sunburst there. The snow is of course somewhat old and very rarely falls all through the summer and so every day the piste basher flattens and breaks up what snow there is, making it nice and hard. This makes it painful on the feet but after a few hours the snow will begin to thaw in the heat of the sun and you will want to take some of your clothes off! At that point the sun will have done its job so well that the snow will start melting and begin reacting in a similar way to blancmange which isn't much good for skiing.

So generally summer skiing entails an early start, limited skiing and not a lot of time to get much done. You must also stick to the marked pistes unless you want to fall down a bottomless crevasse into the glacier. You have to go up high to reach the glacier and for some that can be painful on the ears, eyes, nose and throat because of the thin air. But then again there are a lot of good things to say about summer skiing. For a start it isn't very common yet and not many people do it. When I was in Zermatt last year the pistes were virtually empty, especially early in the morning.

The weather is usually great and very warm which means that you can ski in shorts and a T-shirt by midday. However, it is bitingly cold early in the morning and you must never risk being caught up there with only a few articles of clothing for protection. The more lecherous skier, though, can have a field day skiing behind some of the beauties in their summer ski suits! But, you also have to be careful of the heat, I skied for four days without a hat and my hair turned yellow and has been dropping out ever since (that's my excuse at least). My friend didn't even wear a headband and just about burnt his ears off and we were both badly sunburnt even wearing the high altitude protection cream. You need to keep all tender skin covered by clothing or by some very strong protection cream which should be reapplied regularly.

Other points in favour of summer skiing are that, unless you're an expert, you're almost bound to be one of the worst skiers in the resort because only the experts and the 'six weeks a year since I was three' Americans are there. This means that there is usually no ski school to run into the back of, and the combination of no ski school and no crowds means no waiting for lifts. The lack of skiers generally can mean better prices in the hire shops though lift prices don't come down much.

As you may have gathered though, some of the advantages can work both ways. With usually no ski school, you will not be able to improve your skiing technique and may, if you're still learning, develop some bad habits. Being the worst in the resort doesn't appeal to some people and another problem for the more physically attractive among us – such as myself – being chased down the piste by hordes of young ladies just because I'm wearing shorts can be a little tiring!

There are very few summer ski resorts and even fewer tour operators that offer holidays in them, in fact I've yet to come across one. Information on the summer ski resorts can be obtained from the national tourist offices (for addresses see page 114). It tends to be expensive to get to the resorts under your own steam and then pricey once you get there. This need not always be the case, however, as while the top of the mountain may be covered in snow and ice, the resorts in the valleys below are nearly always warm, full of greenery and tourist restaurants. You can usually find somewhere to camp out in such resorts, leaving your boots and skis locked up at the top of the mountain, and this will save you a great deal of money.

My visits to summer ski resorts have been by discount rail ticket *en route* to the Mediterranean. Then again several of the resorts are off the main train routes and additional train or coach fares may have to be paid, so even short stays cannot be called economical. But, the extra few days' skiing made the summer holidays a lot more fun and July and August detours into the mountains are definitely becoming more popular. One final inconsequential thought on summer skiing, trees cannot grow on glaciers so the scenery can be pretty bleak.

So what do you think?

Well that's virtually it, so what do you think? If this book has done what it set out to do, you'll now be trying to control your urge to zoom down to the travel agent's and get a holiday booked. Or at least you want to rush down to the travel agent, pick up every ski brochure it has, and spend days examining them, pumping the information into your calculator or computer and working out what the best deal is. Then getting it booked.

Whether or not I've instilled in you a desire to ski, I hope at least I have given you an insight into what it's all about. I can't really remember how I felt about skiing before I first went, it was a school trip and all my friends were going so naturally I wanted to go too. But after my first few hours on skis I was hooked, and I've never looked back since even though it was another two years before my Mummy and Daddy could be called on to cough up the money again.

I'm now a member of a ski club, though that doesn't mean anything very specialist but just a group of people who all ski together for maximum enjoyment and who call themselves a club for the sake of it. There are no qualifications for membership and half of last year's party were complete beginners whom we managed to talk into coming with us. Those of the club that have skied before all started in the same way as me on school trips, or college ski trips, sometimes only to Scotland. Incidentally, the very largest ski holiday organisation (no, not Thomson) includes the company Schools Abroad in its group. More and more schools are offering ski holidays to their pupils, usually at all-in prices, and there's probably no better way to learn than with a bunch of schoolfriends. On the other hand, it's never too late! The incentives are always there for beginners from almost all the package tour operators.

Anyway enough of trying to encourage you to go skiing, if I haven't done it yet then I never will. Actually I've never really thought about it before but I suppose skiing must be addictive. What I mean is that no one is paying me to tell you that you should try skiing so I can't see why I'm so keen on promoting the sport. The truth is, of course, that skiing is habit-forming, demanding its own form of religious dedication from which preachers such as me emerge who see it as their mission to convert others to the joys of the world of white. I'm hooked and I want you to be too.

One aspect of skiing that I rather regret leaving out is the world of 'ski talk'. Although there is a glossary of skiing terms, I haven't really told you the sort of conversation often indulged in during the early evening with a complete stranger. So here are a few ideas for great conversation starters:

'Did you know it takes seven minutes to boil an egg up here?'

'Eighty per cent of Austrian skiers drink too much for their own good!'

(That one goes down especially well in Austrian bier kellars.) Follow it up with: 'And 40 per cent of accidents can be attributed to drink.' – and if you do not now have a captive audience try: 'Only 2 per cent of Austrian men don't have a drink while skiing.' You can then branch off into a conversation about alcoholism which is bound ultimately to lead to the introduction of the compulsory seat belt law and drink drive regulations. You can draw the ladies into the conversation with the consolation that a full 11 per cent of the fairer sex don't drink while skiing and perhaps let it develop into an argument on economics about how the Austrians can afford to drink anyway when they charge so much (try this one with the bar tender).

Of course, only the élitist will be able to manage a conversation of this calibre, most are content to keep to the common pastime of discussing the day's skiing with much hyperbole. Jumps, speeds, ski angles and even falls become greatly exaggerated in the skier's mind. It is the done thing to believe whatever ridiculous tales you're told and then when you are in the mood for exaggerating your own abilities, other skiers will look at you with the same wide-eyed excitement you showed them. This rule extends at least as far as all close or distant acquaintances and works especially well in the bar. On the other hand, it is often accepted practice to scorn the more ludicrous story-tellers in the late evening when groups break into couples or threesomes or go to the disco or other similarly exciting events.

When your skiing holiday is finally over, you should have collected a fairly good range of tales to tell the folks back home. You will then be able to enthuse to your heart's content on the merits of the ski holiday to non-skiing friends. If you can persuade one of them to go with you next year you'll find that you are already far in advance of them, and able to look back on your learning days as if they happened some time in the last century.

You may have noticed that no sooner have I got you home from your holiday than you're looking forward to next year's. That's the way it is with skiing, there's no, 'well that's the holiday over for a year'. Even as you start the journey home, the planning begins for next year's holiday based largely on the information you've gleaned from other skiers on which are the best resorts. You have between three and six months to wait only for next year's brochures and during that time you can watch *Ski Sunday* for most of the time and keep up-to-date with clothes and equipment with regular visits to your local ski stockist. Then before you know it, you're leafing through the new brochures, waiting the few months after you've paid your deposit until you're off again, improving your skiing and then it's over again, but not really.

The worst part of the ski holiday must be the end. I remember when I first went skiing, and a few times after, trying to cram in as much as possible into the final afternoon. Not stopping once, just skiing on and on and finishing in the early evening, the last to reach the top with miles to ski down to the bottom. I just bombed down – or the best I could with only six days' experience, it seemed pretty fast at the time. It was almost heartbreaking to take the boots off for the last time and stack them with the others in the ski hire shop. Now things are different, I don't go all out to fit as much as possible into the last day, but I just feel a bit sad making the final lift descent. Now I know I'll be back again next year or even later in the season.

The end of the holiday is when you swap addresses and find out that you mysteriously can't get as much into your bag as when you came, despite the fact that at least one glove and one sock are missing. Most importantly, walking out of the hotel or apartment is the second most likely time you'll fall over and break your legs – the first is walking into the hotel when you arrive.

On the coach everyone waves goodbye to the hotel staff and the courier allows himself to be showered with kisses and wave goodbye to you. He'll be pretty generous with his farewells because the first thing that happens after you get going is the old questionnaire. That's to ask exactly what you thought of the holiday. The form will be divided into sections and will give you a topic like 'Food' and you'll be asked to score from one to five or something like that. This is your chance for revenge! Most companies analyse the results of the questionnaires on the computer and work out averages for different periods and so on.

All that's left is getting the photos back, when you get the unpleasant shock of realizing just how bad your posture was. You can't show them to the neighbours. Never mind you'll just have to take a better camera next year, one that blurs the image so that you look as if you're travelling at speed.

At least it was worth it. See you next year!

Glossary of skiing terms

Aerials, Ballet and Moguls
All these go together to make 'Freestyle'. If you're standing next to someone who screams 'Hot Dog' as another skier shoots past you with one leg in the air and reading a copy of *The Times*, you can turn round to the former and say, 'No my man, that was an aerial ballet actually'. You will then feel vastly superior until you trip over your skis while trying to walk casually away with your nose in the air.

Avalement
The style of skiing where you crouch so low that you are almost touching your knees. It reduces wind resistance and is useful for skiing the dreaded moguls in which case it is known as 'swallowing the mogul'.

Ballet, see Aerial.

Bender Zee Neez
Italian/French/Austrian/Swiss/German/Bulgarian/Spanish/Romanian/Yugoslavian and just about universal translation of the English 'Bend your knees'. This is the most frequent instruction given by any ski instructor to his pupil.

Bindings
These keep the ski boot fixed to the ski. Nowadays most bindings are safety ones that automatically release the boot from the ski in the event of a dangerous fall. At least, you hope they will. Bindings are constantly being modified and improved and are becoming safer and safer. However, they are only effective if they are correctly fitted and checked regularly.

Birdsnesting
American term for skiing off-piste among the trees; a pretty lethal pastime for all but the experts. Never follow James Bond through a wood on skis.

Blood Wagon
Another tasteful American term, this time for the sled used for carrying injured skiers to hospital.

Chalet Maid
Unique young ladies, usually in their twenties, who know more about everything important in the world than any other human being.

Christiania Legere
A French method of turning which involves keeping the shoulders in line with the rest of your body when turning, unlike in counter rotation. When you start learning how to traverse a slope your instructor will nag you to keep your upper body facing downhill while bending and turning your knees to change direction and absorb bumps. You will find this very difficult at first, and will tend to turn your shoulders round too when changing tack. Don't worry, though, it will come to you eventually but a good excuse is just to tell your instructor that you're practising the *Christiania legere* technique and he will either be impressed by your initiative or mark you down as a smart aleck!

Counter Rotation
Or 'the way it should be done'. A technique for turning whereby the skier's shoulders keep facing down

the slope while the hips and legs make the manoeuvre.

Delta, Dendix, Nylon, Snomat and Skimat
Different types of artificial or dry ski slope surfaces. Dendix is by far the most common and could be called the traditional artificial surface.

Edging
Angling the edges of your skis into the slope to stop you sideslipping when you don't want to. The amount of edge you use is proportional to the steepness of the slope.

Egg Position, see Tuck Position

Fall Line
The straightest and usually fastest route downhill.

Federation International de Ski (FIS)
International Ski Federation(!) The world governing body of the sport.

Free Skiing
Term given to skiing unaccompanied by instructor or group.

Gondola
Large cable car ski lift.

Graduated Length Method or **Ski Evolutif**
A method of learning to ski which was invented simultaneously in France by Robert Blanc and in the United States by Cliff Taylor in the 1960s. Beginners start on skis about 1 metre long and move onto longer skis over a period of days until normal length has been achieved. See also page 17.

Gunbarrel
Normally a straight, narrow, fast and dangerous ski run, rather like a bob-sleigh run with sloping sides.

Herring Bone
A technique for climbing uphill; the ski tips are splayed outwards and the skis edged inwards in a sort of inverted snow plough. You then walk.

Hot Dog
A bit of fancy skiing that most of us do by accident. If you hear anyone say it while you are on the piste, duck.

'I flew into some powder up to my neck and it took them an hour to dig me out'
Roughly translated means: 'I can't ski powder and fell over on my first attempt, but as I'm too conceited to admit my failings I lay around in the snow for five minutes at least to make my fall look impressive.' If the person is talking to you at the time then just nod and say sympathetically, 'Oh how horrible/terrible/amazing,' and follow it up with a remarkable story of your own about how you jumped out of a stationary tele-cabine from 20 feet up and then skied down the sheer mountainside so deep in the powder that you needed a snorkel. Then start thinking of an even more incredible tale to counter the one he'll come out with.

Inside Ski
When you traverse a slope with the skis parallel and side on to the gradient, the inside ski is the one nearest the gradient or the 'uphill' ski. If you are skiing properly, all your weight should be on the outside ski (the downhill ski) and you should be able to lift your inside ski from the heel. If you lift it so that the front is higher than the back, your weight isn't far enough forward. If this still sounds confusing, try this simple test when traversing: put your weight on each ski in turn while travelling in the same direction – if you put your weight on the inside ski, you'll fall over.

Kickturn
A method of changing direction while standing still. The skier places his downhill ski upright on its square end and swings it right round and down until it is facing the opposite direction to the other. Then the second ski is

brought round in the same way. Make sure that you don't end up pointing downhill, either forwards or backwards, the consequences don't bear thinking about!

Langlauf
The German and most popular word, as used in many brochures, for cross-country skiing. It is also sometimes called Nordic skiing. The 'loipe' is the track followed by the cross-country skier.

Mogul Field
A lot of moguls ganging up on you to make you fall over, and usually succeeding – in my case at least!

Moguls
Strange man-eating monsters that disguise themselves as miniature hills on a piste, then gang together to make you fall over. They are also described as 'bumps' which is possibly a more accurate, if less terrifying description because firstly they make the piste look like it's got bad acne and secondly you usually get bumped when you hit one and fall over.

Mogul skiing, see aerials

Nylon, see Delta

Parallel Skiing
Skiing and turning with your skis together rather than in a snow plough position. The better a skier you become, the closer your skis will come together as your natural sense of balance and control increases.

Piste
Many a fresh skier has been made to look very silly by rushing off to the bottom of an abandoned ski slope at 8 p.m. after thinking he heard his friends say, 'We're off to the piste', when in fact they said, 'We're off to get pissed (this also works the other way at 8 a.m.). It's an easy mistake to make but a piste is supposedly an area of snow that has been artificially flattened by a piste basher. If you are not skiing on this area, you're skiing off-piste which can be dangerous.

Piste Basher
Large tractor-like machine used for flattening pistes and best avoided when skiing.

Poma, T-bar, Tele-cabine
Different types of lift, see pages 72 to 79.

Ski Evolutif, see Graduated Length Method

Skimat, see Delta

Ski Stoppers
U-shaped sprung clips with prongs that are attached to bindings and spring out if you fall and whenever the boot is not fixed to the ski. They dig into the snow and stop the ski running away and also always seem to get caught together when you're trying to disconnect your skis from one another after taking them out of storage.

Snomat, see Delta

Snow Cat
More boring name for piste basher.

Snow Plough
The beginner's skiing style whereby the skis are positioned in a V-shape with the heels pointing outwards and the tips inwards. The edges of the skis are turned into the slope to help control your speed. To turn and stop by turning into the gradient, you put more weight on the relevant ski. As you become more proficient you will move onto parallel skiing.

T-bar
A type of drag lift, see page 76.

Tele-cabine
A small cable car seating up to eight people, though more often two to four. See also page 79.

Tramlines
Ruts cut into the snow by constant use of the same area of snow by skiers.

Usually found under drag lifts and on narrow tracks and again best avoided.

Traversing
Skiing across a slope to reduce the gradient.

Tuck or Egg Position
This is the pose you will try to copy on your first one-degree slope when it seems as if you're going really fast. Head down, sticks tucked under your arms and pointed up behind you. This creates minimum wind resistance.

Waist and Shovel
The front and middle sections of the ski respectively.

Wipe Out
Crash.

Appendices

1 Useful addresses

British Alpine Racing Ski Club
Coneycroft,
Towpath,
Shepperton,
Middlesex
(09322 21796)

British Association of Ski Instructors
(Ski Teachers 'Union')
Inverdruie Visitors Centre,
Inverdruie,
Aviemore,
Invernesshire PH22 1QH

British Ski Club for the Disabled
Corton House,
Corton,
Warminster,
Wiltshire BA12 0SZ
(098-55 0321)

British Ski Federation
(membership benefits)
118 Eaton Square,
London SW1W 9AF
(01-235 8227/8)

Combined Services Winter Sports Association
(membership benefits)
(c/o British Ski Federation, see above)

English Ski Council
(membership benefits)
Area Library Building,
The Precinct,
Halesowen,
West Midlands B63 4AJ
(021-501 2314)

Hill Publications
(good ski guide magazines, other ski products)
FREEPOST,
Esher,
Surrey KT10 8QS

Inside Edge
(magazine)
Inside Edge Ltd,
8 Bernard Terrace,
Edinburgh
(031-688 2173 or 01-494 0044)

London Nordic Ski Club
c/o Mr Field (Chairman),
21 Dinorben Road,
Fleet,
Hampshire

Ocean Publications
(Ski book sales and ski magazine subscriptions)
22–24 Buckingham Palace Road,
London SW1W 0QP
(Book Order Department
FREEPHONE 2499)

Scottish National Ski Council
(membership benefits)
110A Maxwell Avenue,
Bearsden,
Glasgow G64 4BR
(041-943 0760)

Ski
(American ski magazine)
All American Media Ltd,
54 Burton Court,
London SW3
(01-730 3592)

Ski Club of Great Britain (SCGB)
(membership benefits)
118 Eaton Square,
London SW1W 9AF
(01-235 4711)

Ski Council of Wales
(membership benefits)
PO Box 3,
Chepstow,
Gwent NP6 6NJ
(029-12 71222)

The Skier
(magazine – subscription)
59a Oakfield House,
Hill Avenue,
Amersham,
Buckinghamshire

Ski International
(free magazine sent to everyone on the mailing list, published by the organisers of the *Daily Mail* Ski Show)
Exhibition House,
Lordswood Industrial Estate,
Chatham,
Kent ME5 8UD

Ski Special
27 Belsize Lane,
London NW3

Ski Survey (published by Ski Club of Great Britain)

Ulster Ski Council
(membership benefits)
16 Upper Green,
Dunmurry,
Belfast,
Northern Ireland

The Uphill Ski Club
(skiing for the disabled)
12 Park Crescent,
London W1N 4EQ
(01-636 1989)

National Tourist Offices

National tourist offices will provide free information on resorts and will tell you how to get there using the national transport system. They are well worth getting in contact with for extra resort information when you've made your booking or when you're thinking of making a booking in a resort which you don't know how to get to or if it's worth it . . .

Andorran Delegation in Great Britain
63 Westover Road, London SW18
(01-874 4806)

Austrian National Tourist Office
30 St George Street, London W1R 0AL
(01-629 0461)

Bulgarian National Tourist Office
18 Princes Street, London W1R 7RE
(01-499 6988/9)

Canadian High Commission
Canada House, Trafalgar Square,
London SW1
(01-629 9492)

French National Tourist Office
178 Piccadilly, London W1V 0AL
(01-491 7622)

Italian National Tourist Office
201 Regent Street, London W1
(01-439 2311)

Norwegian State Travel Bureau
21/24 Cockspur Street,
London SW1Y 5DA
(01-930 6666)

Romanian National Tourist Office
77/81 Gloucester Place,
London W1H 3PG
(01-935 8590)

Spanish National Tourist Office
57 St James's Street, London SW1
(01-499 0901)

Swiss National Tourist Office
Swiss Centre, 1 New Coventry Street,
London W1
(01-734 1912; group travel 01-734 4576)

United States Travel and Tourism Administration
22 Sackville Street, London W1
(01-439 7433)

West German National Tourist Office
61 Conduit Street, London W1
(01-734 2600)

Yugoslavian National Tourist Office
143 Regent Street, London W1
(01-734 5243)

2 Dry ski slopes in the UK

Please note, this list includes the location of the dry ski slopes only. For further information on times of opening, size and type of slope and so on, please contact the Ski Club of Great Britain or contact your nearest centre

Greater London, Surrey, Kent, Sussex

Alexandra Palace Ski Centre
Alexandra Park, London
(01-888 2284)

Crystal Palace National Sports Centre
Norwood, London
(01-778 0131)

Blue Sky Hillingdon Ski Centre
Park Road, Uxbridge
(0895 55183)

Woolwich Ski Slope
Greenhill Terrace, Woolwich, London
(01-856 5533 extn 853)

Sandown Ski School
Sandown Park, More Lane, Esher
(78 65588)

Bishop Reindorp School
Larch Avenue, Guildford
(0483 37373)

Folkestone Sports Centre
Radnor Park Avenue, Folkestone
(0303 58222)

Bowles Ski Centre
Eridge Green, Tunbridge Wells
(089 26 4127)

Eurosport Slope
67A North Road, Brighton
(0273 688258)

North Brighton Adult Education Centre
Carden Avenue, Patcham, Brighton
(0273 558897)

The Borowski Centre
New Road, Newhaven
(07912 5402)

Berkshire, Hampshire, Oxfordshire

Carters Ski Centre
99 Caversham Road, Reading
(0734 55589)

Stainforth Ski Centre
Hurst Road, Aldershot
(0252 25889)

Calshot Activities Centre
The Spit, Calshot, Southampton
(0703 768732)

Southampton Ski Slope
Basset, Southampton
(0703 768732)

Brize Norton Ski Centre
RAF Brize Norton, Carterton
(0993 842924)

Gloucestershire, Somerset, Devon

Gloucester Ski Centre
Matson Lane, Robinswood Hill, Gloucester
(0452 414300)

Wellington Sports Centre
Corams Lane, Wellington
(082347 3010)

Exeter & District Ski Club
Clifton Hill Sports Centre, Exeter
(0392 211422)

Wessex Ski Club
Pontins, Barton Hall, Torquay
(0803 25576 day, 33427 night)

Essex, Hertfordshire, Norfolk, Suffolk

Basildon Ski School
Aquatels Recreation Centre,
Cranes Farm Road, Basildon
(0268 3377)

Warley Ski Centre
Warley Gap, Brentwood
(0277 211994)

Harlow Ski Centre
Hammerskjold Road, Harlow
(0279 21792)

Bassingbourn Ski Club
Bassingbourn Barracks, Nr Royston
(0480 77363)

Herts Ski Centre
S & L Sports, 4 St Albans Hill,
Hemel Hempstead
(0442 3755)

Watford Ski School
Woodside Playing Fields,
Horseshoe Lane, Watford
(092 73 676559)

Welwyn Garden City Ski Slope
Gosling Stadium, Stanborough Road,
Welwyn Garden City
(96 31056)

Norfolk Ski Club
Whitlingham Lane, Trowse, Norwich
(0603 650442)

Suffolk Ski Club
Bourne Hill, Ipswich
(0473 686321)

Northamptonshire, Nottinghamshire

Skew Bridge Ski Club
Northampton Road, Rushden
(0933 55808)

Carlton Forum Ski Slope
c/o Golf Range, Foxhill Road,
Carlton, Nottingham
(0602 872333)

Staffordshire, Shropshire

Birmingham Ski Schools
c/o 18/19 Snowhill, Queensway,
Birmingham
(021-236 6816)

Haden Hill Ski Centre
Halesowen Road, Cradley Heath
(0384 633833)

Tebbutts
42 High Bullen,
Wednesbury, Birmingham
(enquiries: 35 Market Place,
021-556 0802)

Telford Ski Slope
Court Street, Madeley, Telford
(0952 586791)

Cheshire, Lancashire, Merseyside

Oval Sports Centre
Old Chester Road, Bebington
(051-645 0551)

Lancaster and Morecambe College of PE
Morecambe Road, Lancaster
(05624 66215 extn 50)

Pendle Ski Club
Clitheroe
(0200 25222)

Ellis Brigham Manchester Ski School
Corner Greengate and Chapel Street, Manchester
(061-834 0161)

Ski Counthill
Counthill School, Counthill Road, Oldham
(061-678 4055)

Ski Rossendale
Haslingden Old Road, Rawtenstall, Rossendale
(0706 228844)

Cumbria, Tyne and Wear, Yorkshire

Carlisle and District Ski Club
Edenside, Carlisle
(022 876 562)

West Cumbria Ski Club
Edenside School, Cleator Moor, Workington
(0946 810306)

Silksworth Ski Slope
Silksworth Lane, Sunderland
(0783 229119)

Catterick Indoor Ski Slope
Loos Road, Catterick Garrison
(0748 833788)

Harrogate Ski Centre
Hookstone Wood Road, Harrogate
(0423 55457)

Scotland

Kaimhill Ski Slope
Kaimhill Playfield, Garth Dee Road, Bridge of Dee, Aberdeen
(0224 38707)

Stoneywood Ski Slope
Stoneywood Outdoor Education Centre, 105 Stoneywood Road, Bucksburn
(0224 712462)

Ancrum Outdoor Education Resource Centre
10 Ancrum Road, Dundee
(0382 60719)

Irvine Valley Ski Slope
High Street, Newmilns
(0563 25628)

Fife Institute of P & RE
Viewfield Road, Glenrothes
(0592 771770)

Drambuie Ski Slope
Aviemore Centre
(0479 810310)

Hillend Ski Centre
Biggar Road, Edinburgh
(031-445 4433)

Loch Rannoch Hotel
By Pitlochry, Kinloch Rannoch
(08822 201 extn 109)

Jedburgh Dry Ski Slope
Jedburgh Anna Complex, The Anna, Jedburgh
(083 56 2566)

Glasgow Ski Centre
Bellahouston Park,
16 Drumbreck House, Glasgow
(041-427 4991)

Polmonthill Ski Centre
Polmont Farm, Polmont
(0324 711660)

Wales

Plas y Brenin National Centre for Mountain Activities
Capel Curig
(069 04 214)

Kelsterton College
Connah's Quay, Deeside
(0244 81753 extn 269)

Cardiff Ski Centre
Fairwater Park, Fairwater, Cardiff
(0222 561793)

Reg Bateman Travel Service Indoor Ski Slope
1 Prince of Wales Road, Swansea
(0792 460358)

Pontypool Ski Centre
Pontypool Park, Pontypool
(049 55 56955)

Black Mountain Ski Slope
Newcourt, Three Cocks, Brecon, Glasbury
(049 74 285)

Northern Ireland

Craigavon Golf & Ski Centre
Turmoyra Lane, Silverwood, Lurgan, Craigavon, County Armagh
(076 22 6606)

PE Centre
The Queen's University of Belfast, Botanic Park, Belfast
(0232 661111 extn 4317)

Ulster Ski Club
Llewellyn Avenue, Belfast
(0232 641326)

Eire

Ski Club of Ireland
c/o Dublin Sport Hotel, Kilternan, County Dublin
(0001 895893)

3 Major ski tour operators in the UK

Balkan Ski Holidays
Carrington House,
126–130 Regent Street,
London SW15 1SF
(01-434 1632)
Specialize in Bulgarian-based holidays. Competitive prices.

Bladon Lines
56/58 Putney High Street,
London SW15 1SF
(01-785 2200)
Up-market resorts and up-market prices in most European resorts and the United States. You have to be pretty to travel with Bladon Lines if their brochure is anything to go by!

Blue Sky
Blue Sky House, London Road,
East Grinstead, West Sussex RH19 1HU
(0342 28211)
One of the biggies and competitively priced to get there.

Club 18-30
24–28 Oval Road, London NW1 7DE
(01-267 6157)
'Only the good die young,' the amount thrown into an 18–30 holiday therefore leaves you dead or exhausted, but either way this is the fun holiday.

Contiki
7 Rathbone Place, London W1P 1DE
(01-637 2121)
You can ski with Contiki for five years longer than Club 18–30 but you'll need to like Austria a lot because that's the only place they go. You'll also need to be rich because Contiki are for the richer 'young' skier. If you are one, they'll take you to New Zealand in the summer.

Crystal Holidays
Alexandra House,
138–140 Alexandra Road,
Wimbledon, London SW19 7JY
(01-879 0535)

Back to long addresses and the mass-market ski companies. Crystal is one of the most competitive companies with some good beginners' offers and bargain trips to France and Austria.

Edwards Ski Holidays
861 Green Lane, London N21
(01-360 7135)
Based in Austria and Italy this smaller company has much to offer, with truly 'all-inclusive' holidays (tailored for beginners) from around £200.

Enterprise Wintersports
1 Wardour Street, London W1V 3HE
(01-439 7611)
Back into the top ten volume carriers, I would say Enterprise are slightly more interested in value for money than low cost. Their holidays have two good features in the form of pre-bookable ski packs and insurance included in the price.

Global Ski
Glen House,
200 Tottenham Court Road,
London W1P 0JP
(01-323 3266)
Back to competition time and Global have a lot to offer, with comprehensive packages and a choice of six countries, plus the best luxury coach travel I know of (some sort of Volvo – also used by Neilson and Ski Lovers). But they could do with some more ski guides and a more comprehensive snow guarantee if they want to progress up the chart.

Hards Wintersports
20 High Street, Solihull,
West Midlands B91 3TB
(021-704 5222)
Competitive prices again thanks to the unique travel method of taking you from London to your resort by coach, excepting the cross-channel bit where they flip you from Lydd airport (near Portsmouth) to Paris (if you're going to Italy or France) or Ostend for Austrian destinations. What will they think of next?

Horizon
Broadway, Edgbaston Five Ways,
Birmingham B15 1BB
(021-643 2821)
Here's another company that includes insurance in the basic price which the other companies don't have much excuse for not doing, particularly those that make their own schemes compulsory. Like Enterprise, Horizon seem more value for money orientated than bargain bucket style and have a policy of not reducing prices to fill seats shortly before departure, as generally practised, which can be annoying when everyone else has had to pay more when booking early. Horizon will also fly from the East Midlands which is more than most can manage.

Hourmont Total Ski
Brunel House, Newfoundland Road,
Bristol BS2 9LU
(0272 426961)
I've acknowledged in this book those who were on a Hourmont ski holiday some years back, it was then a college holiday and Hourmont are probably best known for their school party trips. I won't say anything about that holiday except to say it wasn't the tour company that made it. Hourmont still take you to La Polsa (not much skiing there), I'm not sure if the hotel will still be full of kids, but if Pete is still doing the disco that's worth going for!

Inghams (including Swans)
329 Putney Bridge Road,
London SW15 2PL
(01-785 7777)
Recently celebrated their fiftieth anniversary of taking skiers abroad. This means they were around when only the rich could afford to travel, and some might argue that only the rich can afford to travel with Inghams now. Although this isn't the whole truth, the company is certainly more up-market than most. One of the larger tour operators, covering over 50

resorts of which many are more or less exclusive to Inghams, in eight countries.

Intasun Skiscene
Intasun House, Cromwell Avenue, Bromley, Kent BR2 2AQ
(01-851 3321)
One of the newest of the big boys, Intasun are rapidly expanding and producing quite a tasty brochure offering holidays in the four main ski countries and the potential new number five – Spain. Intasun give some free children's holidays which few others can offer and they must save a bit of money by changing so little of their brochure from one year to the next – savings which are passed on to you in good value and comparatively low-cost holidays.

Marlboro' Adventure Travel
PO Box 36, Thorpe Wood, Peterborough
(0733 50223)
Not always that adventurous, this holiday package licensed to Thomas Cook offers holidays in Austria and Lapland; the latter destination might suit Contiki travellers with a £1000 left over from their first Austrian trip.

Neilsons
International House, Granby Street, Leicester LE1 6FD
(0553 554646)
Neilson claim to be the number one name in skiing, and if that means providing the most services then I have to agree. They have the best snow guarantee I've come across, and a £50 money back guarantee in certain resorts if you don't enjoy skiing after a couple of days. General Neilson policy seems to be that if they haven't introduced a scheme themselves, then they'll do it better than everyone else. Not always the case mind, but they're getting there!

Pegasus Gran Slalom
24a Earls Court Gardens, London SW5 0TA
(01-370 6851)
Along with CITALIA, Pegasus specialize in Italian ski holidays. They mainly go to beginner and intermediate standard resorts, with better class accommodation than the average at bigger than the average price.

Phoenix
29 Thurloe Place, London SW7 2HP
(01-581 4674)
At the time of writing, this specialist in Yugoslavian holidays was still on a high from the 84 Winter Olympics in Sarajevo (you remember – the one people forgot to boycott and Klammer forgot to race in). Pretty good value but fairly limited skiing, so probably best for beginners.

Ski Bonne Neige
24 St Michael's Road, London SW9
(01-326 1005)
According to my CSE grade two French this means 'Ski Good Snow', but at least writing it in French does get the message across that you're only going to go to one resort – Courchevel. Holidays for the bourgeoisie I would say with nasty little schemes like 5 per cent surcharges if you don't pay for the whole holiday when you book. Not as impressive as the resort.

Ski Nat
Holiday House, Domestic Road, Leeds LS12 6HR
Nice prices, with free kids' holidays at times and a pretty lively *après ski* package for the younger skiers, but beware of up to 10 per cent surcharges and airport taxes over £10. But then again late bookings can save you 25 per cent. You pays your money and you takes your chance!

Skiscope
Grosvenor Hall, Bolnore Road, Haywards Heath, West Sussex RH16 4BX
(0444 459921)
'Ski n Fun Parties' and 'Ski Saver Flexi Centre/Season' which used to give us all a cheap laugh (reading them if not indulging) are gone, but Skiscope still offer good 'Direct Sell Holidays at Budget Prices' in Bulgaria, Spain and the four main countries.

Ski Sunmed
4–6 Manor Mount, London SE23 3PZ
(01-699 5999)
At the time of writing Sunmed were giving the best group discounts around, four for the price of three in some chalets. But though they're a little more select than some, the prices are not expensive.

Ski Supertravel
22 Hans Place, London SW1X 0EP
(01-584 5060)
Claim to be the number one, though exactly in what respect is left to your imagination, except of course they have the best: resorts; choice; travel arrangements; service and early booking discounts. I'm not sure I can wholly agree, but I'm not always right!

Ski Thomson
1st Floor Reception, Greater London House, Hampstead Road, London NW1 7SD
(01-387 8484)
The true number one in terms of volume (nearly twice as big as its nearest ski market competitor) and the length of the office address. As the biggest, they cover a large cross-section of the ski market, from bed and breakfast pensions to top-class hotels, and a big variety of resorts too, fifty in five countries (the big four and Spain). I think success speaks for itself.

Thomas Cook
PO Box 36, Peterborough PE3 6SB
(0733 502200)
Similar to Thomson but smaller, including the address (something which you'll learn to appreciate when you write a lot of letters). Better children's discounts than Thomson too, but be careful you don't accidentally get booked onto a Marlboro Adventure Travel holiday as they use the same postbox.

Yugotours
150 Regent Street, London W1R 6BB
(01-439 7233)
Skiing in Yugoslavia – surprisingly enough. Good prices but the resorts aren't quite as Olympic standard as the operators would have you believe.

The Others

(Some of the more original offerings of destination and ski type)

Ski Skills
12 Ranelagh Road, Redhill, Surrey RH1 6BJ
(0737 67152/60429)
Ski Skills offer a unique course of intensive tuition called 'Inner Skiing' which, according to the brochure, helps to make you believe 'skiing is fun'. The idea of Inner Skiing is to get individuals to overcome their fears or negative ideas about skiing – be it fear of bad weather, dislike of queuing or even the cardinal sin of being bored with skiing! The means of curing your inhibitions (whether you think you have any or not) includes discussions, film shows and playing games. The idea of the game playing is that skiers concentrate so hard on pretending to be animals, catching balls, thinking they're a motor bike and so on, that they reach the bottom of slopes which might have worried them, in a way that might have

worried them, in a time that probably will worry them. Prices are not much more than the normal ski holiday package, and Ski Skills go a bundle on trying to get your booking, with follow-up letters to your initial inquiry and so on.

Powder Skiing in North America
c/o Tessa and David Brooksbank,
61 Doneraile Street, London SW6 6EW
(01-736 8191)
The closest I've got to Canadian powder-skiing is a video. It's described as the ultimate skiing experience, and involves being taken up into the vast Canadian snow fields by helicopter and skiing down through endless virgin powder snow. This type of ski holiday has come to be the chief goal of most ski fanatics and certainly something I hope to do in the next decade. Of course the holiday is expensive, and you need to be a very good skier before you attempt it, but I'm sure it will give value for money, and more! It's just getting the valuable money that's the problem.

Tailor Made Ski Tours
Erlysmead House, Farleigh Wick,
Bradford on Avon BA15 2PZ
(0225 859598)
According to one of the founders of Tailor Made Ski Tours: 'The programme is virtually decided and planned by the customer, not by the company. All we do is make it work smoothly.' I would imagine that this is something of an understatement because when I tried to organize a party of six to fill an apartment in Les Arcs with everything already done except paying for it, I managed to find enough problems to keep me in nervous-breakdown condition for six months. The idea of Tailor Made Ski Tours is to give as much flexibility to the skiers as possible. It's the ultimate in personal touch and is largely centred around the resort of Davos in Switzerland. As you might expect it costs a little more than the average ski hol, but you pay for what you get!

Snowtime
23 Denmark Street,
London WC2H 8NA
(01-836 3237/9)
While writing this book I've looked through literally hundreds of brochures: fat ones; thin ones; big ones; small ones, even foreign ones which are easier to understand than you may imagine. Of all the brochures I've seen, I can honestly say that in my opinion, Snowtime is by far the best designed. It is colourful, with good photographs and legible, clear print. Believe it or not easy to read print is a remarkably rare thing in a brochure. The cover shot on the brochure, a picture of a hunky snowsurfer rather than a pretty girl for a change is absolutely brilliant. It's a pity that by the time this book comes out it'll be last year's brochure – perhaps they'll reissue it. I also like their sweatshirts.

However, I haven't included Snowtime just to enthuse about their brochure and sweatshirts. Snowtime, founded in 1978, concentrate their operation exclusively on the resort of Meribel in the heart of the Trois Vallees in France – reputedly the 'world's best resort'. As a relatively small company Snowtime can offer a personal service, with directors in the resort all season; but this doesn't stop them from providing agreeable extras such as unlimited 'free' wine bottled under their own label. I would describe Snowtime as slightly up-market, but their prices are competitive, offering good value for money.

4 Further country, company and resort information

'There are three kinds of lies; lies, damned lies and statistics.'
Benjamin Disraeli

Well that rather grand title and reassuring quote simply mean that I decided to spend another rainy Sunday scratching my head and getting cross studying the brochures of the eleven largest ski companies. Anyway in the following chart I have managed to work out the 20 most popular resorts based on how many companies go to them and I have also given a little information on each resort.

Understanding these brochures isn't easy I can tell you! For one thing the countries are never listed in alphabetical order except in the index at the front. For some reason Austria always seems to come near the back with France at the front despite the fact that Austria has more resorts than any other country. Switzerland makes it to the front in the more up-market Inghams' and Bladon Lines' brochures and Spain comes first in Thomson's. Only Enterprise get their abc correct, though Club 18–30 do well and arrange countries in terms of how many resorts they cover in each, starting with the largest. Otherwise the countries are listed according to the sort of image the company wants to put across.

Another problem in deciphering the brochures was the frequent differences of opinion over some of the facts; usually slight but sometimes rather confusing when trying to get an accurate figure. For example, Thomson say that there are 150 km of prepared piste in Les Arcs while Neilson say there are 150 miles which is quite a difference – though clearly one has used the wrong unit of measurement. Thomson's was the only brochure which listed the different types of runs available which I found useful, while Neilson was the only one to give the number of bars, restaurants and discos in each resort.

The top 20 resorts listed in the following chart are the top 20 only in terms of the number of holidays offered at each one by the top eleven companies. Just as big doesn't always mean beautiful in ski companies, popular doesn't mean the best resorts. Certainly Meribel, which offers some of the best skiing in the world in the Trois Vallees, hasn't made it to the top 20, neither has the most famous St Moritz nor the nearly as famous Val d'Isère, both of which are visited by Bladon Lines. Bladon Lines is the only sizeable company to offer holidays in St Moritz and only Thomson and Bladon Lines go to Val d'Isère. Bladon Lines is also the only company in the top eleven to offer holidays in the United States. The top eleven companies offer holidays in ten countries: Austria; Bulgaria; France; Italy; Lichenstein; Romania; Spain; Switzerland; Yugoslavia; and the United States. From those countries you have a choice of 108 resorts in total, so if I live to be 128, I could do one a year! Perhaps two a year gives me better odds, I've skied in more than ten of them already (phew!).

Of those 108 resorts, 93 are in the main four countries of which 40 are in Austria – a fact I found quite amazing.

Of those 108 resorts, 45 are exlusive to one of the companies in the top eleven, in particular to Inghams and

Thomson. Between all of them the companies offer 292 alternative holidays in the 108 resorts of which nearly half (137) are to Austria, and as you'll note in the chart, nine of the first twelve resorts are in Austria.

As for the chart itself, I must first point out that it is based on the 1984–85 season's brochures so the companies' resorts may now have changed, the facilities may have altered slightly and no doubt the prices will have gone up! So please doublecheck these figures with the new brochures. I have given the height of each resort because the weather at the lower resorts is less reliable and the snow may have melted on the lower slopes by the end of the season. On the other hand, the higher slopes can prove painful on the ears, eyes, nose and lungs because of the thinner air. I've only experienced this once, at 13,000 feet in Zermatt, but friends have been affected at lower altitudes so this is clearly a matter of personal physique.

The cost of equipment hire is for skis and sticks only, boots will cost half as much again; few of the brochures give boot hire charges. The final column, 'ski standard suitability according to Thorne', is based on the common belief that there is little point in paying out a lot of money, if you can't ski, for a lift pass covering hundreds of miles of piste nor to hire top-quality equipment. The two exceptions in this chart are Avoriaz and Les Arcs where you can pay for the superb **ski evolutif** method of learning separately from the hire, tuition and pass and they are therefore ideal places to learn. Please note, however, that just because a resort is said to be best suited to intermediate or advanced skiers, it doesn't mean there isn't a perfectly good ski school for beginners. Likewise the beginner and intermediate resorts often have a great deal to offer the more advanced skier.

Resort	Country	No. of companies in resort	Thomson	Neilson	Inghams	Blue Sky	Horizon	Global	Intasun	Enterprise	Thomas Cook	Club 18–30	Bladon Lines	Black Runs (Advanced)	Red Runs (Intermediate)	Blue Runs (Learner)	Length of pistes (miles)	Number of lifts	Cost of lift pass	Equipment hire price (skis and sticks only)	Resort height (feet) (snow range)	Mountain restaurants	Number of bars	Discotheques/clubs	Ski standard suitability according to Thorne!
1 Kitzbühel	AUSTRIA	10	✓	✓	✓	✓	✓	✓	✓	✓	✓	✓	—	7	19	22	112	57	£50	£12	2500–6500	28	20	8	All standards
2 Mayrhofen	AUSTRIA	10	✓	✓	✓	✓	✓	✓	✓	✓	✓	✓	—	3	9	4	19	23	£45	£12	2000–7000	9	7	6	Beginner/intermediate
3 La Plagne	FRANCE	9	✓	✓	✓	✓	✓	✓	✓	✓	—	—	✓	7	58	15	110	80	£50	£19	6500–10,500	10	21	10	Intermediate/advanced
4 Westendorf	AUSTRIA	9	✓	✓	✓	✓	✓	✓	✓	✓	✓	—	—	2	8	8	25	14	£35	£11	2500–6500	8	6	3	Beginner/intermediate
5 Avoriaz	FRANCE	8	—	✓	✓	✓	—	✓	✓	✓	✓	—	✓				400	180	£50	£24	6000–7500	15	10	3	All standards
6 Bormio	ITALY	8	✓	✓	✓	✓	✓	✓	✓	✓	—	—	—	2	12	6	49	25	£40	£9	4000–10,000	8	14	3	All standards
7 Seefeld	AUSTRIA	8	✓	—	✓	✓	✓	—	✓	✓	✓	✓	—	1	6	8	15	17	£45	£11	3500–7000				Largely beginners
8 Sölden	AUSTRIA	8	✓	✓	✓	✓	✓	✓	✓	—	—	—	✓	9	30	6	110	24	£55	£12	4500–10,000	10	15	6	Intermediate/advanced
9 Söll	AUSTRIA	8	✓	✓	✓	✓	✓	✓	✓	✓	—	—	—	3	23	31	62	53	£40	£11	2000–6000	35	10	3	All standards
10 Obergürgl	AUSTRIA	7	✓	✓	✓	✓	✓	✓	—	—	—	—	✓	10	9	11	62	21	£50	£12	6000–10,000	8	3	10	Intermediate/advanced
11 Alpbach	AUSTRIA	6	✓	—	✓	✓	—	✓	✓	—	—	—	✓	2	5	2	17	18	£30	£11	3500–6000	4			Beginner/intermediate
12 Niederau	AUSTRIA	6	✓	—	✓	—	✓	✓	✓	✓	—	—	—	2	16	28	23	32	£45	£10	2500–6000	8			Beginner/intermediate
13 Sauze d'Oulx	ITALY	6	✓	✓	✓	✓	—	—	✓	✓	—	—	—	5	28	8	75	95	£40	£8	5000–8000	28	20	3	All standards
14 Zell Am See	AUSTRIA	6	—	✓	—	✓	—	—	✓	—	✓	✓	✓				45	24	£45	£9	2500–6500	14	15	8	All standards
15 Cervinia	ITALY	5	✓	—	—	✓	✓	—	✓	✓	—	—	—	5	16	11	140	36	£50	£11	7000–11,500				Intermediate/advanced
16 Chamonix	FRANCE	5	✓	—	✓	✓	—	—	—	—	✓	—	✓				400	180	£50	£18	3500–12,500				Intermediate/advanced
17 Les Arcs	FRANCE	5	✓	✓	—	—	✓	—	—	✓	—	—	✓	15	22	8	150	58	£50	£22	5000–9000	5	5	3	All standards
18 Livigno	ITALY	5	—	—	✓	✓	✓	✓	✓	—	—	—	—				75		£45	£8	6000–9000	6			All standards
19 Saalbach	AUSTRIA	5	—	✓	✓	—	✓	—	✓	—	—	—	✓				118	55	£50	£14	3500–7000	25	9	8	All standards
20 St Anton	AUSTRIA	5	✓	—	✓	✓	—	—	✓	—	—	—	✓	34	70	30	150	70	£55	£15	5000–9000			10	Intermediate/advanced

5 Recommended reading

As I said at the start of this book, there is little if any reading matter as useful as this particular volume! However, for ski technique the best and the most popular book around at present is probably *How We Learned to Ski* by Ali Ross and Harold Evans (Collins in association with Peter Stuyvesant Travel and Channel 4 Television). You may remember that Channel 4 produced a television series of the same name from which an instructional video became available.

I don't go a bundle on these learn to ski books and, though I have nothing like the technical knowledge of the above authors in skiing skills, I don't fully agree with some of the things included. For example, the author's claim that those who have not had at least four one-hour dry ski slope sessions before they go to the land of snow: 'Keenly get into boots for about eight hours a day and often find the skin around the ankles and shins will not take the strain; they may at least lose three days off the skis.' I can see this happening to one wimp in a thousand, but surely it isn't that common? And I certainly disagree with the claim that those who have not had four hours on a dry ski slope 'waste four or five days of an expensive holiday'. If an hour on a dry ski slope is equivalent to a day in the Alps, why bother wasting money going out there – let alone paying for tuition!

However, I'm being too critical, I'm sure the authors of *How We Learned to Ski* could tear this volume to shreds if they wished (and if they had the strength, which looks quite possible in Ali Ross's case). For basic technique the book is well worth taking a look at with good writing, photography and diagrams. Judging by what the skiers wear in the photographs, where they ski and what they do on holiday, the book seems to be aimed at people with an unlimited bank balance. But we poverty-line skiers still use the same ski techniques even if we're at the Skegness of International Skiing wearing the Asda Price of Skiing Fashion. 'Waste not, want not', that's what ten million grannies used to say.

How We Learned to Ski has its own recommended reading list and I was surprised not to see my favourite book on ski technique included in it. It is called *Ski with the Big Boys* and was written by Stu Campbell (who may now wish to remain anonymous) and published by Winchester Press in 1974. On the inside flap of the jacket, the blurb about the book reads:

'Who's a Big Boy? He's the one you turn your head to watch as you ride up the mountain in the chairlift the one whose grin of total pleasure as he flashes past stirs up a painful mixture of envy, understanding, and admiration in your soul . . . the one who can not only get down any slope (after all, you can do that) but can do it in style.' All good stuff of course, but the moral tone of the book rapidly deteriorates and by page 7, something is going badly wrong when the author begins talking about mastering the style of the Big Boys:

'If you are a lady, keep reminding yourself to look sexy. Every woman knows what this means. Men don't so much. While you're skiing pretend that for some reason you want to look especially alluring. Tuck your pelvis in, pulling your fanny and tummy in at the same time. If you look sexy you are probably in a great skiing position*.' *(On the floor in the nude?)

'If you are a man and your fanny sticks out . . .' (See a doctor.)

Seriously though, the book does offer a lot of practical advice on ski technique as do a multitude of others you should be able to find in the sports section of your library.

Barry Waters' *Piste Again* (Queen Anne Press, 1982) is a lot more entertaining than *Skiing with the Big Boys* and indeed it's supposed to be. Even though Barry Waters' efforts are concentrated on the funnies rather than on the practicalities, the book easily manages to give at least 100 per cent more practical information than any other I've come across. Of course the book does make a common mistake in places, which I regret to say that I've found in some of the other books I've looked at, and that's failing to agree with me. For example, in one of his 'rules of skiing' sections, Barry Waters makes the preposterous claim that falling over isn't fun! However, if you don't worry too much about such occasional inaccuracies, this book makes excellent and useful reading. It's my favourite and it's one of the cheapest.

By far the most informative book I've discovered on the library shelves though, has to be *The Guinness Book of Skiing* by Peter Lunn (Guinness Superlatives, 1983). This is an extremely comprehensive guide to the sport giving both ancient and modern history, a wealth of statistics and facts on all aspects of the sport – the sort of thing you would expect to find in a Guinness book – plus a lot of straightforwardly presented information on ski technique. You'll also find a slightly more serious look at the danger of avalanches than I could manage. It really contains some excellent stuff for the skier and, apart from the sections on ski technique, it tells you how to deal with different snow types, different pistes, different weather conditions and so on – which most ski books tend to miss.

The author's grandfather and father were responsible for inventing the downhill and slalom races respectively, and a good deal of other things, including the first World Championships and the first ski holiday tour. Peter Lunn himself has been an accomplished skier, of international standard, for the past 60 years!

Getting in Shape to Ski by 'American Citizen' Tage Pederson (Kaye and Ward, 1970) is one of the best ski fitness books I could find. It has easy-to-follow instructions and diagrams of simple but effective exercises for the skier before, during and after the holiday. Tage Pederson was the official trainer to the American ski team in the 1968 and 1970 World Championships. As the book was published some years ago, you'll probably only be able to find it in the library.

Useful in a different sort of way and more interesting to read generally was Elizabeth Hussey's *The Greatest Ski Holidays* (Proteus, 1982) which gives good statistical information as well as Elizabeth Hussey's personal evaluations of ski resorts all over the world, including many of the major European ones. I found it interesting to look at the authoress's opinions on resorts, though I wouldn't visit one just on someone else's recommendation and regardless of price etc. An extremely interesting and well-written book.